CLOSE YOUR CHURCH FOR

VOLUME 1

THE DEATH AND RESURRECTION OF THE CHURCH

A CALL FOR THE CHURCH TO DIE SO IT CAN RISE AGAIN

JEREMY MYERS

The Death and Resurrection of the Church:
A Call for the Church to Die so it Can Rise Again

Published by Redeeming Press
Dallas, OR 97338
RedeemingPress.com

ISBN: 978-1-939992-01-7 (Paper)
ISBN: 978-1-939992-02-4 (Mobi)
ISBN: 978-1-939992-00-0 (ePub)

Learn more about Jeremy Myers by visiting RedeemingGod.com

JOIN JEREMY MYERS AND LEARN MORE

Take Bible and theology courses by joining Jeremy at
RedeemingGod.com/join/

Receive updates about free books, discounted books,
and new books by joining Jeremy at
RedeemingGod.com/reader-group/

TAKE THE *SKELETON CHURCH* ONLINE COURSE

Join others at
RedeemingGod.com/join/
and get all my courses for free, including
"The Skeleton Church" online course:

GET EBOOKS AND THEOLOGY COURSES AT REDEEMINGGOD.COM/JOIN/

Thanks for reading!

Books in the *Close Your Church for Good* Series

Preface: Skeleton Church

Vol. 1: The Death and Resurrection of the Church

Vol. 2: Put Service Back into the Church Service

Vol. 3: Church is More than Bodies, Bucks, & Bricks

Vol. 4: Dying to Religion and Empire

Vol. 5: Cruciform Pastoral Leadership

Books in the *Christian Questions* Series

What is Prayer?

What is Faith? (Forthcoming)

Can I Be Forgiven? (Forthcoming)

How Can I Avoid Hell? (Forthcoming)

What are Spiritual Gifts? (Forthcoming)

How Can I Study the Bible? (Forthcoming)

Other Books by Jeremy Myers

Nothing but the Blood of Jesus

The Atonement of God

The Bible Mirror (Forthcoming)

The Re-Justification of God: A Study of Rom 9:10-24

Adventures in Fishing for Men

Christmas Redemption

Why You Have Not Committed the Unforgivable Sin

The Gospel According to Scripture

The Gospel Dictionary

All books are available at Amazon.com

Learn about each title at the end of this book

For all who follow Jesus
outside the four walls
of Christianity

ACKNOWLEDGEMENTS

As always, special thanks go to my wife, Wendy. She is my biggest fan, my most faithful reader, and the one who catches typos in articles I have read ten times. She is more beautiful every year, and always asks tough theological questions which I can rarely answer.

I also want to thank those who read my online articles at RedeemingGod.com. Many of the ideas in this book have already been posted there, and the comments and insights left by readers have challenged, encouraged, and inspired me to refine the ideas in this book.

A final thank you goes to Ward Kelly for proofreading this book and for providing many valuable suggestions.

TABLE OF CONTENTS

CHAPTER 1

THE SATANIC CHURCH

"The criticism of religion will prove to be the most beneficent historical incident in the history of Christianity since it became Christendom."
—Vincent Cosmao

Imagine that a satanic church exists in your town. Though they have never done anything overtly satanic that you are aware of, certain people in the surrounding community are uncomfortable with such a church operating in their town and want the church to shut down.

The church members argue that they have the right to exist just as much as any church, and to prove it, they embark on a community relations campaign to improve their public image. They change their name to "The Church of the One World Hope." Their services begin to copy those of a typical Christian church. They meet on Sunday mornings. They sing songs. They listen to an encouraging sermon by one of their leaders. They even start "outreach" programs for the community. They host an after-school program for children, and volunteer down at the homeless shelter. Some of their members serve on school boards or get elected to the city council.

Slowly, the voices of protest fade away, and over time, people forget that the church had satanic influences. The church is accepted among the other various religious groups in the community, and is allowed to coexist with them. For a while, the church actually becomes the most prominent church in town. It has the largest building, the most people, and the biggest budget. It gains power, prominence, and authority. Nothing, it seems, can slow its growth.

How would you respond to such a church? What would you think about its continued existence? Would you hope and pray for such a church to close?

YOUR CHURCH

The shocking truth is that such churches do indeed exist in most of our communities. We don't realize these churches surround us because they are not blatantly satanic. As was described in the scenario above, these churches do not look satanic, act satanic, or appear satanic. In fact, most of the members of such churches are not aware of the satanic influences, history, and values that are present in the church they attend.

And how could they? The satanically influenced church has become so normal today, it has become mainstream. These churches are not hidden from sight. Many of us may drive by such churches every day on our way to work or when we pick up our children from school. We all have friends and neighbors who go to such churches. Some of us even attend one.

Yes, the church I described above may even be *your church.*

Now before you get too angry at such an outrageous statement, hear me out. I don't for a second believe that Christian churches are actually worshipping Satan when they sing about Jesus, pray to Him, or teach the Scriptures. And no, this is not another book which condemns the Catholic Church as the Great Whore, or the Seeker Sensitive Church for compromising the gospel, or the Emergent Church for succumbing to postmodernism. I am not condemning any denomination, doctrinal distinctive, or particular type of church as "satanic." My concern is much more basic than that. My concern is not with any *form* of church, but with the institution of "church" itself.

I believe that nearly every church in America—no matter which denomination, no matter how large or how small, whether they meet in a cathedral or a house—has adopted certain values, practices, and goals which are not in line with the ways of Jesus, but find their origin instead in the values and goals of the Deceiver. Though we believe we are following the ways of Jesus, we are instead following the ways of Satan.

And yes, this includes the church I am part of as well. The church I am part of is not faultless in these areas. We too have adopted satanic values and influences. None of us in any of our churches worship Satan, follow Satan, pray to Satan, or read the satanic Bible, but we are still, in a sense, "satanic."

How?

Well, when we recall that *satan* is Hebrew for "adversary," then any area in which we act *adversarial* to the ways and values of Jesus is, by definition, "satanic."[1] In other words, to the degree in which we adopt the values and goals of Satan rather than the values and goals of Jesus, to this same degree we are more like

[1] See the lesson on "Satan" in my "Gospel Dictionary" online course. Visit RedeemingGod.com/courses/ to learn more.

Satan than we are like Jesus. Any practice or value that is contrary to the ways of Jesus and His Kingdom, or brings harm to the cause of Christ and damage to His name, it could be said that these values and behaviors are satanic. If in our lives or in our churches we adopt values and behaviors that are contrary to the will and ways of God, then these areas are, by definition, satanically influenced.

Such an idea is not as shocking as it sounds. If Peter himself could be called "Satan" by Jesus when Peter tried to deny the purpose of Jesus in going to Jerusalem to die (Matt 16:23), then it is no different to think of churches as having adopted values and goals that also are contrary to the values and goals of Jesus.

What is more, John, in writing the book of Revelation, begins the book by pointing out how several of the churches have lost their love for Christ, and are tolerating immorality and idolatry. One of these gatherings he even calls "The Synagogue of Satan" (Rev 3:9). Were they worshipping Satan and doing satanic activities? Probably not. To the contrary, this "Synagogue of Satan" probably taught and worshipped in the name of Jesus, just like any church today. But for the Apostle John, the values and goals of this gathering betrayed them. Though they likely met and worshipped in the name of Jesus, this particular fellowship had adopted satanic values and goals, and so John called them out on it.

Others have proposed similar ideas. In his groundbreaking synopsis of Revelation 2–3, Walter Wink points out that the message to the seven churches is actually the message of Jesus to seven angels. He writes this:

> It is the *angel* who is held accountable for the behavior of the con-

> gregations, and yet the congregation is virtually indistinguishable from the angel. ... Far from being perfect heavenly beings, these angels encompass every aspect of a church's current reality, good and bad alike.[2]

Such an idea seems benign enough, until we realize that much of what Jesus says to some of the angels makes them sound more like demons than angels. The angel of Ephesus has left its first love, and is described as having fallen, and is called upon to repent and return to doing good works, lest Jesus come and remove its lamp stand (2:4-5). The angel of Pergamum is tolerating idolatry, sexual immorality, and the beliefs of the Nicolaitans, which Jesus hates (2:15-16). So also, the angel of Thyatira allows a female false prophetess to teach, to commit sexual immorality, and to worship idols (2:20). Some have even gone to the depth of Satan (2:24). In light of all of this, Wink states that:

> The angel of a church becomes demonic when the congregation turns its back on the specific tasks set before it by God and makes some other goal its idol. A church with shrinking numbers may become obsessed with growth and the recovery of its former glory. A minister with a dominating personality may attempt to impose the program that worked so well at her or his last church. None of this may sound evil in itself, but ... it can be disastrous.[3]

In a sense, John points out to all seven churches in Revelation 2–3 where they are failing to follow Jesus, but have instead adopted values and behaviors that are contrary to Jesus—values that are

[2] Walter Wink, *Unmasking the Powers: The Invisible Forces that Determine Human Existence* (Philadelphia: Fortress, 1986), 71-72.

[3] Ibid., 78.

satanic. Yet John's purpose in writing to the seven churches was not to condemn, but to redeem; not to destroy, but to deliver.

And that is the goal of this book also. Scripture teaches that the whole world is under the control of the evil one (1 John 5:19). While the church is supposed to be salt and light, a city on a hill, leading the world toward righteousness and justice, we have far too often allowed the world to influence and mold us into its pattern—the pattern of the devil. The world has done to the church what instead the church must do to the world.

Part of the problem is that the church has often failed to recognize the relationship that exists between the church and the world.

THE CHURCH IN THE WORLD

When it comes to the church's relationship with the world, everybody tries to fulfill the prayer of Jesus in John 17:13-16 that His followers would be in the world but not of the world. The various ways that Christians have tried to live this out runs the gamut.

On the one hand, there is a whole group of Christians who believe that other than living on earth, we should have as little to do with the world as possible. Individuals and groups such as these often retreat into caves or communes where they can spend their days praying, reading the Bible, and interacting only with other believers. The desert monks in the early centuries of the church were of this sort, as also are many of those who dwell in monasteries and convents. In today's world, some Christians retreat into Christian communities where they live, work, and interact only with other Christians. Sometimes they do this by moving off into actual communities where everybody lives, eats, and works. But more frequently this is done by Christians attempting to only make friends with Christians, attend activities where only Christians will be present, only work at "Christian" jobs, only tune in to Christian radio and Christian television, and only read Christian books.

Those who live this way must be commended for their attempt to keep from being polluted by the world, but it seems that they have partitioned themselves off from the world to a much greater degree than Jesus Himself ever did. Jesus was constantly accused of being a friend to tax-collectors and sinners (Luke 7:34). He was accused of being a glutton and a drunkard because of who He hung out with (Luke 7:34). But is there any danger of anyone accusing this first type of Christian of being a friend to sinners, prostitutes, and drug-dealers, or of partying too much? No, they are usually so serious, straight-laced, and dour that they kill any party they accidentally walk into, and keep at arm's length anybody who might cause a stain on their sterling reputation (their reputation among Christians, anyway).

This first group has overemphasized the second part of Jesus' prayer—that His followers would *not be of this world*—and have gone to such great lengths of separating themselves from the world that they have lost all opportunity to speak into the world, to be salt and light, or to walk with the world in its suffering, pain, and fear. Like the religious Jews of Jesus' day, in a commendable attempt to be holy and separated unto God, they have completely fenced themselves off from the surrounding society and culture. But as the saying goes, "They are so heavenly minded, they are no earthly good." Though their intentions were sound, they do not reflect the same way of life that is exhibited by

Jesus Himself, and hence, it is safe to say that this way of living is not what Jesus meant in His prayer.

However, on the other extreme are those Christians who seem to have no discernible differences between themselves and the surrounding world. Their actions, beliefs, behaviors, values, goals, language, clothing, and all other aspects of life pretty much resemble and duplicate those of the surrounding culture. The only real difference is that they attend a church service on Sunday morning, and maybe they read their Bible every now and then. But for the most part, they are making absolutely no difference whatsoever among their friends and neighbors, most of whom probably don't even know that this person is a Christian.

This second group has overemphasized the first part of Jesus' prayer—that His followers would *be in this world*—and have gone to such great lengths at joining with the world in its activities and functions that the end result is similar to the result of the first group: they too have lost all opportunity to speak into the world, to be salt and light, and to walk with the world in its suffering, pain, and fear. Like some of the compromising political leaders of Jesus' day, they have so adopted the worldly system, values, and goals that they are often just as trapped in the power struggles and the quest for money and possessions as everyone else. And since they themselves are trapped in this never-ending race, they are unable to help anybody else break free into the values and goals of the Kingdom of God. Like the first group, this second group does not reflect the way of life exhibited by Jesus, and so once again, it is safe to assume that this way of living is not what Jesus meant in His prayer.

Somewhere between these two extremes is the balanced position of *being in the world, but not of it.* Learning how to walk in this balanced way is not easy, and is a large part of what being a Christian is all about. All of us lean to one side or the other, and frequently swing back and forth between the two positions. Sometimes we get tired of the pain and troubles of the world, especially when we experience them ourselves, and so we make the attempt to partition ourselves off from the world. We say we are not going to be "of the world" any longer. We stop hanging out with our non-Christian friends. We throw out our secular music, cancel our cable TV, put up crosses around our house, and attend more Bible studies. This is an easy trap to fall into, and even the Apostle Peter succumbed to this temptation in his ministry (cf. Gal 2:11-21).

Other times, we feel like we want to make an impact in the world, inspiring people to change. This is a good and loving desire. But after a long series of small steps, we find ourselves in a compromising situation at work where we are helping friends siphon off money from the corporate account, or we end up getting divorced because we were never at home, or we feel that to "minister" to our neighbors, we need to keep up with their standard of living and buy the fancy boat, go on the expensive vacation, and get all the newest technological gadgets. Maybe after a while we see the emptiness and foolishness of this sort of lifestyle, and we swing back the other way toward separation from the world.

Following Jesus involves this endless cycle of trying to find the proper balance between being in the world but not of it. To find this middle ground, there are two principles which are helpful to keep in mind. First, Jesus is our perfect guide. As the Christ, He shows us the proper balance between "Christ and Culture." Two of the images He used to describe this balance are salt and light

(Matt 5:13-16). For salt to be effective, it must be in the food, while remaining distinct from it. That is, the salt has to be put into the food, or put upon it. Salt does no good if left in the saltshaker. But at the same time, the salt must remain salty; it must do its job. It must provide the flavor, the seasoning, and the work of preserving. So also with light. For light to be effective, it cannot be in a room filled with light, but must go into the darkness. Yet to be effective in the darkness, it must not become darkness itself, but must shine bright lest it lose its effectiveness of being light. So these images are somewhat helpful in learning to be in the world but not of it.

But when trying to find the proper balance between being in the world and not being of it, it is also helpful to distinguish between the kingdoms of the world and the Kingdom of God. Specifically, we must not think of either the world or the Kingdom of God as "places" but rather as two opposing systems of rules, values, goals, and priorities.[4] When we think of the world and the Kingdom of God in this way, then being in the world but not of it is not about leaving this world entirely, or even about changing most of our outward *actions* and *behaviors.* Instead, being in the world but not of it means abandoning the rules, values, goals, and priorities of the world, and adopting the new rules, values, goals, and priorities of the Kingdom of God. In this way, living *in the world but not of it* is done by living as fully as possible in this

[4] Walter Wink, in his insightful book on how Christians are to live with discernment and resistance in a world of domination, recommends that when Scripture talks about "the world" it is helpful to substitute "the system" for "the world" so that we can better understand what the biblical author is saying. See Walter Wink, *Engaging the Powers: Discernment and Resistance in a World of Domination* (Minneapolis: Fortress, 1992), 58.

world, but according to a different set of values, goals, and principles. To be *in the world but not of it* is to live in this world in the most fully human way possible while not adopting the worldly system founded upon rivalry, greed, accusation, hate, and violence.[5]

When we are in the world but not of it, we still have non-Christian friends, and go to non-Christian places, and do things that non-Christians do, but we make choices, spend money, and decide what (and who) is important in life by using a different set of values than those of the world. Though some of our actions and behaviors may end up being the same as the people of the world, we do these things for different reasons and to accomplish different goals. Our goals and our values must be aligned to the rule and reign of God in our life and the desire to see God's rule and reign expand throughout the entire earth. That is how we live in the world, but not of it.

We live "in the world" by entering into business, community, and friendships with others as much as humanly possible, and we keep from being "of the world" by refusing to accept and adopt its value system. When understood this way, to be *in the world but not of it* is not so much about outward behaviors as it is about values, goals, priorities, and motivations.

Yet it is precisely here where the church has most often gone astray, and where we return to the primary subject of this chapter. By and large, the church has not adopted the values, goals, and priorities of the Kingdom of God, but has instead adopted the values, goals, and priorities of this world. Though many of the

[5] See the lesson on "World" in my "Gospel Dictionary" online course. Visit RedeemingGod.com/courses/ to learn more.

things we do look and sound religious, the values and goals behind these actions more closely resemble the values and goals of the prince of this world, rather than the values and goals of God.

As discussed above, there have been three common ways the church has tried to be "in the world, but not of it." Some churches emphasize the part in the prayer of Jesus where we are to not be of the world, and so have retreated into caves and communes. Others emphasize the part in prayer of Jesus where He wants us to be in the world, and have emulated much of the behavior and practices of the world in an attempt to make an impact or be "relevant." Most churches, however, fall somewhere between these two extremes.

But whichever of the three approaches is taken, almost all churches have adopted the system, values, priorities, and goals of the world, which turn out to be the values and goals of Satan as well. This is just as true of monastic communities as it is with the people who meet in lavishly-constructed cathedrals. It is true of mega churches and home churches. It is true of conservative evangelical churches and liberal mainline churches. It is not the methods, the size, the traditions of our church that make us more like Jesus, but the motivation and priorities by which we function. And it seems that almost all churches, of all sizes, from all denominations and creeds, have adopted the values, goals, and principles of this world. And since the values and goals of the world originated with Satan, we can say that almost all of our churches are satanically influenced.

THE CHURCH AS A PERSON

The idea that the church has some satanic influences is shocking to some, but it need not be. It helps to think of the church as a person. Whatever is true of an individual Christian can also be true of the church in general. Just as a single person will never be perfect this side of heaven, so also, the church, composed as it is of human beings, will never be perfect this side of the return of Jesus Christ. And just as we, as individuals, can still be influenced, tempted, and led astray by the values and goals of Satan, so also can the church.

No Christian is perfect, and neither is the church. Though theologically, we are "in Christ," the reality of our position in Christ is not always reflected in daily experience. Sometimes, true believers do very evil things. And it must be admitted that all of us still sin. All of us can be tempted and led astray by Satan. All of us can adopt satanic values. All of us can live according to the goals and principles of this world, rather than those of Jesus Christ and the Kingdom of God. We all have certain habits, values, and tendencies which resemble those of Satan rather than Jesus. It is not unbiblical to say that sometimes all of us are influenced to think and behave in ways that have more in common with Satan than with Jesus.

So also with the church. Sometimes, the church behaves in ways that reflect the values of Satan rather than those of God. We still worship Jesus, pray to God the Father in heaven, read and study the Bible, and seek to live a life led by the guidance of the Holy Spirit, but the values and goals of Satan have infiltrated our minds, our practices, and our decision-making processes so that while we think we are living according to the principles of the Kingdom of Heaven, we are in fact living according to the principles and values of Satan, and his kingdom of darkness. Satan has done a relatively good job covering his tracks and masking his influence, but the signs of tampering are everywhere for those who want to see.

A QUESTION OF CONTROL

Ultimately, it comes down to a question of control. As believers, we belong to Christ. We have been bought and paid for by His blood. We are redeemed. The church is the Body of Christ, the Bride of Jesus, the people of God who follow Jesus into the world.[6]

But ownership is one thing; control is quite another. You may own your car, your computer, or your cell phone, but if any of these get stolen, they are completely out of your control. So also with the church. Jesus owns the church, but if we give some of the control to a source other than Jesus, then the church is being influenced by this other source.

So as members of the church, we must ask, "What is it that controls us?" We like to say "the Bible" or "the Holy Spirit," but if we take a serious and discerning look at how our local churches make decisions and what values and goals guide these decisions, a new picture begins to emerge.

This serious and discerning look begins by looking at the world, and asking, "What are the dominant values and goals of this world? Not just in the United States, or in Europe, but across the entire world, and throughout time?" There is one prominent characteristic or value which transcends nations and generations:

[6] For a definition of church along these lines, see Jeremy Myers, *Skeleton Church: A Bare-Bones Definition of Church* (Dallas, OR: Redeeming Press, 2012).

power. Throughout history, everything is about power. The questions are always: Who has the power? How does one get power? Where does power come from? How can we get more power? And what should power be used for, except to get more power?

There is not a characteristic which is more prominent around the entire world and throughout time. Power is desired by governments and corporations. Even small clubs and individuals seek more power. Systems and structures are set up to enforce and maintain the power of those in charge.

Power, of course, isn't necessarily bad. God Himself has power; immense power. He is infinitely powerful. Jesus also is powerful, and He even gave us power to help us carry about our mission in the world (Acts 1:8).[7] The Spirit comes upon us in power. Governments, kings, and authorities have been given power by God to help maintain peace (Rom 13:1-7). So power itself is not bad. It is a good gift of God. But power, just as with any other gift from God, is only good as long as it is used in connection with God and His purposes. Power becomes evil when it is divorced from God. And when power is separated from God, it struggles against God to gain power over God.

This is one of the grand narrative themes of Scripture. In many ways, the Bible is a record of the struggle between the Powers. From the very beginning, Satan sought to gain power and control over God. And when God created Adam and Eve, Satan recruited them for his ongoing struggle. From Genesis 3 onward, the Bible contains the story of the disastrous consequences of

[7] In speaking of the power that God has given to us to carry out our mission, many also point to Luke 10:19 and Matthew 28:18, but the word used in these verses is not "power" but "authority" which is quite different.

mankind's decision to join with Satan in his rebellion against God, and how God has sought to restore our broken relationship with Him. The Bible reveals that God, though He alone has infinite power, uses this power to redeem, reconcile, love, serve, and even humiliate Himself (Php 2:5-8), as He seeks the restoration of all creation. Humankind, however, following Satan's lead, most often uses power to gain more power over others, and to destroy, steal, harm, and lord our position over others.

The contrast could not be clearer. The struggle from time immemorial has been about power: who has the power and how it should be used. God has shown one way of using power and Satan has shown another. Furthermore, it is crystal clear that the mass of humanity has followed the pattern of Satan in our quest for more power and our use of power over others. One of the reasons Jesus came was to show humanity a new way of using power: a way of love, service, and self-sacrifice.

The question for the church then, is "Which pattern are we following? God has given us power, so how are we using it? Which values control our decisions and goals? How does the power we have influence our priorities?" To answer these questions, we must take a detailed look at the ways in which the world has influenced the church, and compare these ways with the values and goals of Jesus Christ. We must compare our use of power with the ways that Jesus used His power and how the devil uses his, and then see which ways most resemble the church. And wherever our values and goals are incongruent with those of Jesus, we must have the courage to take the steps that are necessary to change. We must boldly root out any area where the church has adopted the values and goals of Satan, and redeem and transform these areas so they come to reflect the values and goals of Jesus

Christ instead.

DESTROY THIS CHURCH

It is not an issue of motives. I believe that the motives of most churches are pure. The average Christian church truly does its best to worship God, teach and obey the Scriptures, and help people become faithful followers of Jesus Christ. We truly do seek the Kingdom of God and its righteousness.

However, certain practices and values have crept into the church which are not only contrary to Scripture, but are also contrary to the life and message of Jesus Christ. These practices and values have become so normal and accepted within Christianity that we *believe* they reflect the values of Jesus and the Kingdom of God when in fact they do not. Instead, they more closely resemble the goals and values of the world, the flesh, and even the Deceiver himself.

Walter Wink, in his insightful book, *Unmasking the Powers*, writes about some of the ways the values of this world have infiltrated our churches and usurped our message. Though we claim to live and preach the gospel of Jesus Christ, our actions often betray values and goals that are contrary to those of Jesus Christ. Here is some of what Walter Wink says:

> When television evangelists would try to terrorize us with Satan and then speak favorably of South African apartheid, we should have sensed something wrong. … When evil ran roughshod through corporate boardrooms and even churches, unnoticed and unnamed, while "Satan" was relegated to superego reinforcement of moralistic

scare tactics, then we should have caught the stench—not of brimstone, but of putrefaction.[8]

There is something sad in the moralistic tirades of fundamentalist preachers terrifying the credulous with pictures of Satan lurking in the shadows, coaxing individuals to violate rules which are often enough satanic themselves and deserve to be broken, while all the time ignoring the mark of the cloven hoof in economic or political arrangements that suck the life out of *whole generations* of people.[9]

[William Blake writes:] "Man must and will have some religion: if he has not the religion of Jesus, he will have the religion of Satan, and will erect the Synagogue of Satan, calling the Prince of this World, God, and destroying those who do not worship Satan under the Name of God. ... Every religion that preaches vengeance for sin is the religion of the Enemy and Avenger and not the Forgiver of Sin, and their God is Satan, named by the Divine Name."

Blake is not talking about Satanism ... but about Christian churches that behave satanically under the banner of Christ. To his criterion for discerning satanic "Christianity" we might add these: hostility toward those who are different; projecting evil out on others who are then demonized; claiming doctrinal certitude; breeding psychic dependency, unconsciousness, stagnation, fear, guilt, or hatred; depicting God as a monster (as in ascribing the death of loved ones to God). Satanic Christianity can be rigidly legalistic or morally slack ... But these are characteristics of much of what passes as Christianity![10]

[8] Wink, *Unmasking the Powers*, 9.
[9] Ibid., 28.
[10] Ibid., 36.

> Religion itself with all its trappings—ritual, laws, creeds, doctrines, buildings, calendars, and celebrations—is one of the most virile and deadly of all the *stoichea* (Gal 4:3; Col 2:20), precisely because it lulls us into believing that speaking *about* God is a substitute for relating to God directly.[11]

If Wink is right, then the adoption of satanic values has led us to turn God into an idol. When we share the values and goals of Satan rather than the values and goals of God, our worship and actions reflect these satanic values, even if we name the name of God. In this way, the worship of God becomes twisted and perverted as well, so that we do not engage in the worship of God, but in the worship of a false god, an idol of our own making. We sing and we pray and we give offerings to this idol, thinking that it is God when it is not, because the values and goals we have adopted have nothing to do with the values and goals of the Kingdom of God.

In the name of God—but with the values of Satan—we busy ourselves with religious activity, all the while ignoring—or even condemning—the very things God is doing in the world. This helps explain why the church has so often come down on the wrong side of the social issues of the day. For example, here in the United States, though the pilgrims arrived to this country for religious freedom, we immediately sought to restrict the religious freedom of the people we found here—the Native Americans. Not only that, but we turned a blind eye to the atrocities committed by colonists and by our own government upon the Native American people, and sometimes even encouraged and praised

[11] Ibid., 149.

these activities upon the "pagan" people of this land. It could be argued that the church chose its stance because of the lure of power that came with siding with those in power.

A similar series of events happened with slavery. While a few voices cried out in dissent, the vast majority of American churches defended the practice of slavery and ignored the horrid treatment and inhumane living conditions of African slaves in our country. Even when the Civil Rights Movement broke out, once again, most American churches campaigned loudly and strongly against granting equal rights to African Americans. When the writings and sermons of the pastors who did not support the Civil Rights Movement are studied, it quickly becomes clear that their primary motive was to protect their power, prestige, and position within the community. They did not want to side with those whom they considered weak and poor, for this might require them to relinquish some of their power and authority.

History is littered with examples like this where churches have stood up for the wrong goals and the wrong values, all in a vain attempt to gain or maintain power, prestige, and authority. Which should cause us to wonder ... What are the areas today where we have forsaken God's mission in the world to the poor, the oppressed, and the weak so that we can increase and consolidate our wealth, power, and strength? Where do we no longer worship and follow God, but worship and follow an idol which promises to give us power? These are not easy questions.

But before any of these questions can be answered and before a solution can be sought, we must first discover how we came to adopt satanic values and influences. How is it that the church came to trade the values and goals of the Kingdom of God as taught and lived by Jesus Christ for the values and goals of Satan?

We will look at this process in the next chapter, but let me close this one with a prayerful sonnet from my favorite poet, John Donne. In it, he recognizes that his heart has been taken captive by the enemy, and so he prays that God would attack and batter down the doors of his heart so that he might be free. Though it is not Scripture, this Sonnet is my life prayer, and it has also become my prayer for God's Church.

HOLY SONNET XIV

Batter my heart, three-person'd God; for you
As yet but knock; breathe, shine, and seek to mend;
That I may rise, and stand, o'erthrow me, and bend
Your force, to break, blow, burn, and make me new.
I, like an usurp'd town, to another due,
Labour to admit you, but O, to no end.
Reason, your viceroy in me, me should defend,
But is captived, and proves weak or untrue.
Yet dearly I love you, and would be loved fain,
But am betroth'd unto your enemy;
Divorce me, untie, or break that knot again,
Take me to you, imprison me, for I,
Except you enthrall me, never shall be free,
Nor ever chaste, except you ravish me.

DISCUSSION GUIDE FOR CHAPTER 1: "THE SATANIC CHURCH"

1. What does the author mean when he says that some churches are "satanic"? What do you think of this idea?

2. In Revelation 2–3, what is the Apostle John pointing out the seven churches and why is he pointing this out?

3. What does Jesus really mean when He prays that His followers would be in the world but not of the world?

4. Which part of Jesus' prayer in John 17 do you tend to overemphasize in your life: "being in the world" or "not being of the world"? Why do you think you lean this way and what are some practical changes you can make to restore balance?

5. If William Blake (He is quoted by Walter Wink near the end of the chapter) is correct, then our adoption of satanic values has led us to turn God into what?

Application: History shows that most of the church did not defend the Native Americans or the African Americans from horrible mistreatment, but often used Scripture to *defend* this mistreatment instead. Today we recognize how wrong the church was for doing this, and we say that if we had lived in those days, we would have stood up for freedom, liberty, equality, and justice.

But the truth is that each generation tends to be blind to their own injustices and mistreatment of other people. We are blind because we are both in this world *and* of it. But we can have our eyes opened by asking who it is that our churches most loudly accuse and condemn. This adversarial approach to certain groups of people is *the clearest indicator* that we are listening to the spirit of Satan rather than to the Spirit of God.

So who do you condemn? Who does your church accuse? Is it the homosexuals and the gays? Is it immigrants? Is it Muslims or the military? Is it the Democrats or the Republicans? Is it the President? Whoever it is, ask the Holy Spirit to open your eyes so that you might see them through the eyes of Jesus Christ as someone who is infinitely loved and completely forgiven.

CHAPTER 2

FAITH OF THE FALLEN

"Called on to legitimate the empire, the church abandoned much of its social critique."
—Walter Wink

When I was young, there was a seemingly-simple mathematical story problem that bothered me to no end. It went like this:

> Three men went on a trip, and stopped at a hotel for the night. They went in and asked the clerk for a room. He said it was $30, and so the three men each paid $10, and went up to the room.
>
> However, the clerk realized that he had made a mistake. There was a discount he forgot to apply, and the room should have been only $25. Being the honest employee that he was, he sent the $5 up with the bellboy.
>
> The bellboy, however, was not as honest. He realized that the three men would have trouble dividing the $5 evenly between the three of them, and so he decided to "help" them out by keeping $2, and giving the remainder to the men.
>
> So, each man effectively paid $9 each, for a total of $27. The bellboy kept $2, which brings the total to $29. What happened to the last dollar?

The math is simple, and maybe I am just slower than most, but this problem stumped me for many years. I could not figure out where the math went wrong. Finally, during a trigonometry class in college (yes, I didn't figure it out until college), I realized the mistake. The answer to the problem is that the $2 the bellboy kept should not be added back on to the $27 the men paid, but must be subtracted, bringing the *total paid* down to $25. Based on a little misinformation and misdirection, the story problem asked a wrong question, and led me astray for many years.

In some ways, the same thing has happened to the church. Somewhere, somehow, we have been fed misinformation. This misinformation has led to numerous misleading questions. And these misleading questions have led us to provide wrong answers, which in turn caused the church to adopt harmful values and goals that are contrary to the values and goals of Jesus Christ.

To correct this, we need to go all the way back to the beginning. Before we can correct our values and goals, we need to ask the right questions, and before we can ask the right questions, we need to understand and correct the misinformation we have been given.

MISINFORMATION

The misinformation begins where everything begins: in the Garden of Eden. God created the heavens and the earth, and all the celestial and earthly bodies to fill them. At the pinnacle of creation, God created Adam and Eve. They were given authority to tend the plants and animals, and were instructed to multiply upon the face of the earth. But Satan, in the form of a serpent, was also in the Garden. Satan questioned Eve, challenged the instructions and intelligence of God, and ultimately deceived her and Adam into eating fruit from the Tree of the Knowledge of Good and Evil. As a result, they brought death upon themselves, and a curse upon creation.[1]

For the next several thousand years, the story of Scripture reveals a constant struggle between the plans of God and the perversions of Satan. Whenever God sets something in place, Satan twists and perverts it. In every case, while the creation of God still resembles God's original idea, Satan's perversion accomplishes the exact opposite of God's intent. Every plan and intuition of God is warped, turned, and distorted by Satan so that it *looks* like what God intended, but a*ccomplishes* what Satan desires. The entire Old Testament can be read in light of this ongoing cycle.[2]

Eventually, the new Adam, Jesus Christ, entered history to start afresh and set the story straight. But, as in the beginning with Adam and Eve, Satan tried to turn Jesus away from the instructions and plans of God. Satan used against Jesus the same methods and tactics he used with Adam and Eve. He questioned the word of God and challenged the authority of God. Ultimately, Satan brought three temptations before Jesus. According to Luke 4:1-13, the first temptation was for Jesus to satisfy His hunger by turning stones into bread. In the second, Satan promised to give authority over the nations to Jesus if Jesus would just worship Satan. Finally, Jesus is tempted to perform a great miracle in the sight of the worshippers in the temple courts by throwing Himself from the pinnacle of the temple so that angels would

[1] Listen to the first several episodes of my "One Verse Podcast" for a more detailed explanation of Genesis 1–4. Go to RedeemingGod.com/itunes/

[2] See J. D. Myers, *The Bible Mirror* (Forthcoming).

rescue Him before He struck the ground.

The temptations were not just attempts by Satan to get Jesus to do something contrary to the will of God. On the surface of the temptations, there is nothing overtly "sinful" about them. Satan was not asking Jesus to murder someone or commit adultery. After all, if Jesus was hungry, and He has the power to make stones into bread, where is the harm in that? Later in the Gospels, Jesus turns water into wine at a party and multiplies five loaves and two fish to feed a hungry crowd. Is this first temptation so different? If Jesus could multiply fish and loaves of bread to feed hungry people, and turn water into wine to give people more to drink, what would be sinful in transforming a few stones into bread to satisfy His own hunger?

The same dilemmas exist with the next two temptations. One of the goals of Jesus was to regain authority over the nations of the world. And now it was being offered to Him. Finally, during His ministry, Jesus performed many miracles in the sight of people, and one of the reasons was so that they would recognize Him as the Messiah. What is the problem with one more?

Ultimately, the three temptations were not about the action itself. To the contrary, the actions that Satan suggests are all good and noble actions. If Jesus were a pragmatist—if He thought that the ends justified the means—then there would be nothing to stop Jesus from doing what Satan wanted, for Satan was offering exactly what Jesus wanted. To provide for people's needs, to be recognized as the Messiah, and to become the ruler of this world were all good and proper goals of Jesus, and Satan was offering these three things to Jesus.

But Jesus knew that God's will must be done in God's way. He also knew that there are no shortcuts to accomplishing the will of God. So the reason Satan's temptations would have been sinful for Jesus is not because the outcome was sin, but because the values and methods that Jesus would have to adopt were sinful. They would have accomplished God's will, but not in God's ways or with God's values. To see this, let us look more closely at each of the three temptations.

THREE STRIKES

In the first temptation, the temptation of turning stone into bread, Satan wanted Jesus to act selfishly. Satan wanted Jesus to become self-reliant, self-centered, and to seek His own self-provision. The action itself of turning stones into bread would not have been sinful, for Jesus performs similar actions later in His ministry when He multiplies the loaves and fish. But in those miracles, He is looking out for the needs of others, not for Himself. God's will is done by putting the needs and interests of others above our own. So the first temptation is about selfish individualism. Jesus refused to put His own needs first, and seek to have His own needs met.

The second temptation focuses on authority and power. Satan offered Jesus dominion over the earth. Again, this is not a bad thing in itself. Jesus did have authority and power, and one of the reasons He became a man was to become the world's rightful ruler so that every knee would bow and every tongue confess that Jesus Christ is Lord (Php 2:10-11). This is what Satan offered to Jesus. But to obtain this from Satan, Jesus would have to adopt wrong values and methods. Though Jesus did want to reclaim authority over the nations, He knew that His victory would only come through death and suffering; not through a deal with the devil.

Furthermore, the devil's idea of authority is at odds with that of God. When the devil exerts authority, he does so with money, glory, power, riches, and fame. This is contrary to the quiet and gentle authority of Jesus. So this second temptation is about control. Satan wants to control people. He wants to control the world and the universe. He wants to control God. This temptation was a power grab. In offering Jesus power, Satan positioned himself to gain even more power. Jesus is not opposed to power, but knew that it must be gained through sacrifice and service, and used for the benefit and blessing of others.

Finally, Jesus is offered the chance to receive praise and recognition from men. He is taken to the pinnacle of the temple, and told to throw Himself down so that God would be forced to rescue Jesus by sending angels to catch Him. Since the temple courts were nearly always filled with people, this angelic rescue would take place in the sight of them all, and they would be in awe of Jesus. Many would proclaim Him as the Messiah. They would praise Him and welcome Him. All would see that God was truly with Jesus, watching over and protecting Him. This third temptation was an opportunity to be recognized. It was an opportunity for Jesus to make His name great, and receive His due glory, and to be proclaimed to all the world as the Messiah. Again, there is nothing wrong with the goal. This also is why Jesus came. But as with the first two temptations, the problem was in the methods and values that Jesus must adopt to achieve His goal. Rather than following God's will in God's ways, the method Satan proposed used satanic values to obtain the will of God, which would have ended up not being God's will at all.

So the three temptations were about selfish individualism,

power and control, fame and glory. These were offered by Satan as a means to accomplish the mission of Jesus. Walter Wink asks,

> What is Satan tempting him with here, and in each of these "temptations," if not what *everyone knew to be the will of God?* ... He presents Jesus with well-attested scriptural expectations which everyone assumed were God's chosen means of redeeming Israel. Satan throws up to Jesus the collective Messianic hopes ... Satan offers him, in short, not outright evils but the highest goods known to Israel. This is when the satanic is most difficult to discern—when it offers us the good instead of the best.[3]

Satan offered Jesus the fulfillment of all the prophecies about the Messiah: prophecies about power, might, and empire. But Jesus turned them all down, knowing that such things would not help, but would only hinder the goals of God on earth through Jesus.[4] Jesus knew that if He was to do what God wants, He must also do it in God's ways. Ways of self-sacrifice, service, humility, patience, and love.

FALLING TO THE TEMPTATION

Following this victory over temptation, Jesus began His ministry. He gathered and taught disciples, performed many miracles, and then died on the cross and rose again from the dead. Through His life of service, and especially His death, burial, and resurrection, Jesus gained what Satan had promised, but gained it accord-

[3] Walter Wink, *Unmasking the Powers: The Invisible Forces that Determine Human Existence* (Philadelphia: Fortress, 1986), 18.

[4] For more on Luke 4:1-13, see my online Grace Bible Commentary at GraceCommentary.com.

ing to the will and ways of God; not through selfishness, but through service; not through power, but through humility; not through riches, fame, honor, and glory, but through poverty, weakness, shame, and relative obscurity. And before Jesus ascended to heaven, He instructed His disciples to follow His example, and pass on the training that He had given them (Matt 28:19-20; Acts 1:8).

Over the next few centuries, the followers of Jesus did their best to follow the teachings of Jesus according to His example and values. But it was tough. They faced constant threats from the government and the military. Some of them lost their jobs, their families, and even their lives. They were scorned and ridiculed. And yet as they served and loved others, gave self-sacrificially of their time and possessions, and offered forgiveness and grace when wronged, the message about Jesus continued to spread and lives were changed.

But then something happened. The temptations of Satan came back around. As more and more people became followers of Jesus, the focus of many Christians began to shift. The emphasis began to move away from self-sacrifice, service, generosity, humility, and peace, and toward power, influence, prominence, authority, recognition, and control. This is seen in a variety of ways. Though the motives were to protect and educate new believers, church leaders began to consolidate power and control. They created a hierarchy of religious leaders who helped develop rules of morality and decide which understandings of Scripture were correct. They tried to increase their influence in society by gaining more followers and defending Christian beliefs against the claims of philosophy and other religions.

One of the greatest shifts came when the Roman Emperor

Constantine converted to Christianity after he defeated his enemies under the sign of the cross. As a result of this victory, he declared Christianity the official religion of the Roman Empire. Mass conversions followed. Thousands of pagan temples were transformed into places of Christian worship. Almost overnight, Christianity became rich, powerful, and prominent. It also became a tool of the Empire. The leaders of Christianity blessed the Empire's wars, approved the Empire's laws, and installed the Empire's rulers. In exchange, the Empire gave land, money, and buildings to the church, which only increased the church's power, influence, fame, and worldly glory.

In his book, *The Myth of a Christian Religion*, Gregory Boyd describes the transition this way:

> Once the Church acquired power over others, everything changed. A movement that began by viewing the acquisition of political and military power as a satanic temptation now viewed it as a divine blessing. A movement that was birthed by Christ refusing to conquer his enemies in order to die for them now set out to conquer enemies—for Christ. The faith that previously motivated people to trust in the power of the cross now inspired them to trust in the power of the sword. Those who had previously understood that their job was to serve the world now aspired to rule it. The community that once pointed to their love for enemies and refusal to engage in violence as proof of Christ's lordship now pointed to their ability to violently defeat enemies as proof of Christ's lordship.[5]

[5] Gregory A. Boyd, *The Myth of a Christian Religion* (Grand Rapids: Zondervan, 2009), 25. See also Jacques Ellul, *The Subversion of Christianity* (Grand Rapids: Eerdmans, 1986), 19-68.

Whereas Jesus has turned down selfish individualism, power, control, riches, fame, recognition, and glory as a means of accomplishing His mission, some of the early church leaders fully embraced such things as a means to spread the gospel, fulfill the Great Commission, and expand the Kingdom of God on earth.

FOOL'S GOLD

The rationale is easy to understand. Few of us would have done anything different. The conversion of Emperor Constantine caused persecution to cease and brought in tens of thousands of additional converts. Leaders wanted to protect these new believers from heresy or from other religions. They reasoned that gaining money, power, and buildings made this training and education of the masses more manageable. Also, being the official religion opened the way for the rapid spread of the gospel. None of this seems to be wrong in any way, shape, or form.

And so began what many call the "Golden Age of Christianity." With the money and power gained by the church, it now had the resources to provide for its own needs. It became self-sufficient and could expand in ways never dreamt of before. It became the official religion of the Roman Empire with all its might and power. The church gained authority and glory in the eyes of the people. Its clergy became scholars and philosophers, great men of learning and education. Buildings were constructed and great public works were carried out. Laws were written, rulings were made, and control was gained. The commands of God and the instructions of Jesus became the laws of the land and could be enforced by legal means. All of this resulted in the spread of Christianity, and with it, better government, improved education, and increased morality.

This seemed to be so obviously "of God," what could be wrong with any of it? Only one thing. Somewhere along the way, the very things that Jesus had rejected to accomplish His mission—self-reliance, power, authority, glory, riches, recognition by men, and control—these things were adopted in full force by the church. The Golden Age was filled with Fool's Gold. The very things that Jesus refused, the church accepted. And to the degree that the church sought power, money, control, influence, and public recognition, to that same degree, the church followed the pattern of Satan rather than the pattern of Jesus. "When Satan offers to give him all the kingdoms of earth, Jesus refuses, but the church accepts, not realizing from whom it is receiving the kingdoms."[6]

If there is one thing we can learn about Satan from Scripture, it is that he is a master deceiver. His best deceptions are those that appear to be the will of God, but under the surface are full of the satanic values of selfishness, greed, and ambition. Even when we are apparently doing the will of God as recorded in Scripture, and even when we are seeing godly results of our efforts, there is no guarantee that we are in fact following God rather than Satan. In Matthew 7:22-23, people accurately prophecy and truly cast out demons in the name of Jesus, which are all good works, and according to the will of God, but when they stand before Jesus, He says to them, "I never knew you. Away from me, you evildoers." Such a passage should give pause to every Christian and every church, making them ask, "Am I really doing the will of God?" When seeking to answer this question, we must not say "Yes" too

[6] Ellul, *The Subversion of Christianity*, 124; cf. 125-136.

hastily. For if we seek to accomplish God's will using the values and systems of this world, it might not be following God at all, but something else entirely.

FIGHTING FIRE WITH FIRE

It is often argued, of course, that we must fight fire with fire. The systems of this world and the values of Satan require a response of similar tactics and means. It is almost never phrased in that way, but the language of power and control permeates the church as we preach and teach about how to win against the devil. We need power, it is argued, to fight the power of evil. To defeat evil, we need a show of force. We must strike hard and strike fast. We must make the first hit count.

All this sounds good. It sounds right. It sounds natural. But the Kingdom that Jesus set up is not natural; it is not of this world. It is certainly for this world and in this world, but it does not use the same thinking, values, or methods of this world. "The weapons of our warfare are not carnal," says Paul (2 Cor 10:4). So when the church tries to fight the enemy with the enemy's tools and weapons, we do not defeat the enemy but end up defecting to the side of the enemy. When we fight the powers of evil with the rules and weapons of the powers of evil, we end up fighting on the side of evil itself.

> Engaging a Power on its own terms guarantees that the victor, whichever it is, will perpetuate the same terms. ... Whenever we let the terms of the struggle be dictated by the Power that we oppose,

> we are certain to become as evil.[7]
>
> We must ask how we are like the very Power we oppose, and attempt to open these parts to divine transformation. ... We must discern the spirituality that we oppose and be careful not to grant it victory within ourselves.[8]

This is how churches become satanic. We fight evil with the same weapons and values that are used by the powers of evil. In so doing, we think we are fighting fire with fire, but the powers that be were only too happy to lend us their weapons for when we use such weapons against evil, we are actually fighting on the side of evil itself. When we seek to gain power, money, control, fame, and recognition in our fight against evil, we are not fighting for the cause of the Kingdom of God, but for the values and goals of the kingdom of this world.

The solution, then, is to stop using wicked weapons when fighting wicked forces. When it comes to the Kingdom of God and the kingdom of this world, we cannot fight fire with fire, but must follow the way of Jesus in laying down our lives, sacrificing ourselves for others, and giving up our desires and dreams for the good of others. Only in this way will heaven on earth prevail.

We must not think we can use the weapons of the enemy to defeat the enemy himself. Just as in J. R. R. Tolkein's *Lord of the Rings* Trilogy, men were often led astray into thinking they could use the power of the One Ring to defeat their enemy Sauron. The lure of such immense power caused them to believe that their

[7] Walter Wink, *Naming the Powers: The Language of Power in the New Testament* (Philadelphia: Fortress, 1984), 117, 130.

[8] Ibid., 130.

resolve would remain firm, that their faithfulness to their cause would resist the evil of Sauron. But as Gandalf reminded the nine members of the Fellowship of the Ring in Rivendell, "The Ring answers only to Sauron himself. It has no other master."[9] Sauron is only too happy to let men wear the ring, for when they do, they became his servants, despite any intention they might have had to the contrary.

So also with the church. When we try to use the weapons of our enemy—weapons of power and control—we begin with the best of intentions, but the simple act of wielding these fell weapons lead us to fight for our enemy, for they answer only to Satan. Jacques Ellul gives some specific examples:

> When we see the innumerable efforts for action that the churches make; when we see all the dissertations and "calls to action" and programs; when we see, for instance, that in the political sphere Christians go no further than this ridiculous question: "Are we to act for or against Communism?" ... [or] "Oh, so you're against the machine?" ... or again, "What must we do to change these conditions?" —when we see all this, we cannot help being horrified at this miserable imitation of the world, of the works of the prince of this world.
>
> Christians are so deeply imbued with the fundamental doctrines of this world that they no longer have any liberty of thought or life.[10]

What then can be done? If we cannot use the weapons and tactics of the world to defeat the powers in the world, how then

[9] This quote is found in the movie, not in the book itself.

[10] Jacques Ellul, *The Presence of the Kingdom* (Colorado Springs: Helmers & Howard, 1989), 75.

should we proceed?

THE WRONG QUESTIONS

The way forward begins with noticing that we have been asking all the wrong questions. As indicated at the beginning of this chapter, we can easily be led astray by asking the wrong questions. And far too often, the church has asked the wrong questions. Based on the values that we have adopted from the world and from Satan, the church has come to ask questions about becoming self-reliant, powerful, authoritative, glorious, and rich. Far too often, we seek recognition, control, wealth, and prosperity. We run after influence and leadership and court those with power and prestige.

Since these are our goals and values, we ask questions on how best to accomplish and achieve such things. Questions like, How can we increase donations? How can we gain the ear of the City Council, the Mayor, the Governor, or better yet, the President? How can we influence who fills these offices? How can our church be recognized as the best in our city? How can we fill our parking lots and pews? How can we get our church on the evening news? How can we gain name recognition in our community? How can we get people to notice us?

Such questions are generally asked within the context of a more biblical question: How can we make disciples? This certainly is a great question, and has biblical precedent in the command of Jesus to make disciples (Matt 28:19-20). However, the misinformation we have received from history, tradition, and society has so colored our thinking and the way we read Scripture (especially the Gospels), that even the concept of discipleship has been subverted. Becoming a modern disciple of Jesus rarely involves what Jesus intended. The question of how to make disciples today is often answered in ways that promote the goals of power, control, authority, glory, and riches.

Yet according to Jesus, if we would become His disciples, we must take up our cross, serve others, give generously to those in need, and be willing to suffer and die. Yet in many churches today, discipleship is more defined by doing what the pastor says, giving generously to the church budget, following the rules of the church, and living in a way that does not mar the image of the church in the community. Prayer and Bible reading are often involved, but only as long as they are done in a way that agrees with the doctrinal statement of the church and pads the attendance numbers on Sunday morning and Wednesday night.

Service is also encouraged, but only when it is part of an approved program within the church. Going off on your own to start a ministry is generally discouraged, unless you first receive the blessing from the pastoral staff and elders. And the worst of all taboos is joining another church for their service project. This is because in the subconscious minds of many, making disciples is not so much about turning people into fully devoted followers of Jesus Christ, but keeping control over people within the four walls of their church buildings.

When all this is put together, discipleship today seems to be primarily about filling the pews and the offering plate. "Successful" discipleship looks like multiple Sunday services, massive building expansions, and ever-expanding ministry budgets. Discipleship has been boiled down to attendance, tithing, and serving in church programs.

So when we ask, "How can we make disciples?" what many

are actually asking is, "How can we increase attendance, tithing, and involvement in church programs?" And behind these questions are often the unstated questions from above: "How can we increase our power and prominence? How can we increase our image and influence? How can we get people to recognize us and all the good we do for our community?"

These, I believe, are the wrong questions. We only ask them because we do not know any different and because we have been influenced by a long history of misinformation about what the church is and what the church is supposed to do.

THE RIGHT QUESTIONS

Only once we have discovered some of the wrong questions can we begin to ask the right questions. The first right question that needs to be asked is, "What is the church?" Answering that question, however, requires a complete book of its own. Many have written such books, and I have made my own attempt at developing a bare-bones definition of the church in my book, *The Skeleton Church.* In it, I propose that the church should be understood as "The people of God who follow Jesus into the world." This definition shows that the church consists of God's people or God's family. The church is not a building.

Secondly, I show that the biblical definition of church includes an action, or activity. God did not create the church for it to be passive. The church is to be active. And what does the church do? It follows Jesus. It goes where Jesus goes and does what Jesus does. And where is it that Jesus goes? He never goes to where it is safe and peaceful, but to where the darkness and chaos is greatest. He runs into the flames; not away from them. If the people of God are following Jesus, they too will be led into the places of this world where sin and evil reigns. The church is not a safe place for people to hear heart-warming sermons and heavenly choirs, but is rather the people of God forming a beachhead on the distant shores of a dark country from which we launch rescue missions to those who are trapped within the clutches of evil. This is the church, and this is what the church is supposed to be and do.

Only when we have understood the church in this way can we begin to ask more right questions. Questions about leadership and control. Questions about when and where to gather, or why and how. Questions about what to do with our money, time, and resources. Questions about the role of the Bible and doctrine. Questions about our place in politics and society. These are the right questions to ask.

But seeking answers to these sorts of questions will have to wait for another book. The rest of this book will focus on a simple shift in thinking that can help the church begin asking the right questions. To get back on the path of following Jesus, the church must turn from any area where the satanic values of power, greed, and pride have taken root, and must follow in the way of Jesus. The church must begin to think about its ministry the same way Jesus thought about His. Rather than seeking power, honor, riches, fame, and glory, the church—just like Jesus—must seek death. To truly follow Jesus into the world, the church must die.

DISCUSSION GUIDE FOR CHAPTER 2: "FAITH OF THE FALLEN"

1. What are the three temptations that Jesus faced in the wilderness, and what values or goals do they actually represent?

2. What is one of the primary methods Satan uses to trick us into accepting what Jesus Himself rejected? In other words, in each of the three temptations, what was the one thing Satan offered to Jesus in relation to the will of God?

3. What event in church history was instrumental in causing the church to accept the three things that Jesus rejected during His temptation in the wilderness? Why did the church leaders accept these things?

4. Can power, wealth, fame, and control be safely used by the church to accomplish God's will in this world? Why or why not?

5. Rather than ask how we can get an audience with political leaders, gain power in the corporate world, or acquire influence and fame among entertainers, what questions should we be asking instead? What are your answers to these questions?

Application: Rather than gaining power, influence, wealth, fame, glory, and control, Jesus wants His church to make disciples. And while it seems that power, wealth, and control can be used to help us make disciples, church history shows us otherwise.

So how should the church go about seeking to make disciples? What are the characteristics of true disciple of Jesus, and how are these characteristics exemplified and encouraged in the church? Can they be gained by sitting in a pew every Sunday while singing songs and listening to a sermon?

CHAPTER 3

THE CHURCH MUST DIE

"Death, not life, is God's recipe for
fixing the world."
—Robert Farrar Capon

What would happen to your city if your church building vanished or if it could no longer afford to stay open, and so it sold the building and shut down for good?

Think first of what might happen to the people who attended the church. Most would be sad that their church closed, but the majority would eventually start attending another church in town. A few might stop attending church altogether, but it's safe to say that the lives and schedules of most of the people in your church would change very little. Only the address of where they go to church would change.

How about the people who may not attend on Sunday mornings, but are involved in some of the church programs? If the church has programs like Youth Group, MOPS, AWANA, AA, or a free meal for the homeless on the Second Tuesday of the month, all the people who attend these programs would have to find other churches or social groups to host them. This is generally not too difficult, even in the smallest of towns. I once pastored a church in a small town with a population of 169 people. We were the only church in town, but there were other churches in nearby towns that had nearly identical programs. If our church had shut down, the people who attended our programs simply would have gone to another church or community center that hosted similar groups.

Moving outward from the church a little further, there are the immediate neighbors of the church—those who live next door to the church building, or on the same street or block. Would they notice if your church shut down? Sure. But how much would it affect their lives? Most churches have surprisingly little contact with their closest neighbors. If your church closed, the neighbors might wonder what happened, but there would likely be little noticeable difference in their lives. The only exception to this would be if your church was the "rude" neighbor on the block. Some churches do not make the best neighbors. This is especially true of large churches in residential areas. Police and pastors often receive complaints from the neighbors of large churches about traffic congestion and excessive noise on evenings and weekends. Just as you would probably be annoyed if a large dance club opened up next to your home because of the noise and traffic it would cause, so also, many neighbors get annoyed by large churches on their street. So in these cases, the neighbors might actually rejoice if your church closed.

How about the other people in town? Would the residents even know your church was gone? Again, it probably depends on the size and prominence of the church, but in general, your church closing down would generate little more than gossip and speculation. Would the city council care? The Police Department? The Mayor? How about the gangs, prostitutes, and drug dealers? Would the media notice? Would the closure of your church make the nightly news? Would the newspaper write an article? Even if they did, would it be a leading story? They might do a report if your church was a historic landmark, but probably only if your town is small. Old churches close all the time, and the media rarely gives them even a few lines of news. The only other time church closures get reported is when a mega-church closes because a pastor or staff member are caught in a sex scandal or financial crime.

So tragically, the only people who would really notice that your church closed are the people who attend there and the pastors of the other churches that would receive them. This is true for far too many churches. The average person in your community and neighborhood would only know that your church shut down because the "For Sale" sign went up. The brutal truth is that if your church closed, the negative impact on the surrounding community would be minimal at best. Most may not even notice.

Why is this? The church is to be a beacon of hope in the darkness, a city set on a hill, the salt that preserves society and culture. But are we really any of these things if the average person in our neighborhood wouldn't notice if we closed up shop? What has happened that the church, which seeks to be light and salt in the world, has become so insignificant and marginalized?

PUBLIC RELATIONS

Many believe the primary problem is one of image and perception. We are misunderstood, they say. Our hearts and motives are pure, and we want to help people learn and live the truth of the gospel. But for some reason, the average person on the street has a negative perception of the church. They read about church corruption and pastoral sex scandals in the newspapers, and they don't trust us. Many have tried attending a church, but got burned, or became tired of being asked for money. As a result, the average person on the street thinks the church is greedy, hypocritical, unforgiving, judgmental, harsh, and selfish.[1]

If you attend a church, it is likely you do not agree. Most churchgoers believe the opposite of what the person on the street believes. People who attend church believe their fellowship is warm, friendly, gracious, generous, compassionate, and kind. So when we hear that non-churchgoers believe we are rude, arrogant, selfish, greedy, and mean, we get a little defensive. We are shocked at how we have been misunderstood. We are certain that if these people visited *our* church, they would see how wrong they are. We are convinced that they would like church if they just came to ours. While it might be true that they had a bad experience in another church or as a kid when they were growing up, things are different now. Our church is not like those other churches.

Ironically, our loud (and sometimes abrasive) denials rarely help. Telling people who do not go to church that they are wrong about the church usually only confirms their convictions that we are rude, arrogant, unloving, and never really listen to anybody but ourselves. It is like an abusive husband and angry father being told that he is mean and hurtful, and his only defense is, "I am

[1] See for example: Dan Kimball, *They Like Jesus, But Not the Church* (Grand Rapids: Zondervan, 2007); Dave Kinnaman and Gabe Lyons, *unChristian* (Grand Rapids: Baker, 2007).

not! I'm kind and caring!" He might be convinced by this logic, but nobody else is.

So we're stuck. We believe we are kind and loving, but the watching world believes the opposite. We further believe that the only reason they think what they do is because the church is misunderstood and misrepresented. It is only the Christian kooks who make the news, and most Christians are not like these crazy cult leaders. We believe that if the average person on the street would just attend church, they would see how warm and loving we Christians really were.

But here we are faced with another dilemma. How can we get people to visit our church if they don't trust churches in general? People won't come to church when we invite them unless they first begin to change their perceptions about the church. How can this be done if we can't get them to attend? We need them to attend so they can change their view of the church, but they won't even visit a church unless they first change their opinion.

Typically, a church faced with this dilemma embarks on a public relations campaign borrowed straight from the pages of Corporate America's User Manual. When Toyota recalls millions of cars for sticky gas pedals, they simultaneously air commercials on television about all the safety awards they have won. When a BP oil rig spews oil in the Gulf, Florida rolls out advertisements about how their beaches are still safe and clean. When the antenna on the new iPhone doesn't work properly, Apple sends all users a coupon for a free case.

So churches do the same thing. To counteract our negative image in the public arena, we develop slogans like "First Community Church: The Perfect Church for People Who Aren't" or "Grace Church: A Hospital for the Hurting." Then, once the image and slogan are developed, the public relations campaign really begins in earnest. People are invited to "come as they are," and are reminded that "We're all sinners on the road to change." Signs and banners are displayed around the church so the members understand (and hopefully live) what is taught. Sermon series are preached on the themes of forgiveness and love. Air time is purchased on television and radio to run commercials about how great and loving our church truly is.

Then we sit back and wait for the people to arrive so we can *really* begin to show them how loving we are.

The problem, however, is that the public relations campaign doesn't always work. In many cases, the perspective of outsiders only gets worse.

LAWN TRASH

In my first year as a pastor, our church was struggling to raise attendance. We decided that part of our problem was that the community was not aware of our presence. We were tucked off on a side road in town, a road on which few people drove. We had a visibility problem. So to correct this, we went with a smorgasbord approach. Members went out and knocked on doors to invite people to church. We sent out mass mailings. We hung flyers on people's doorknobs. We left CDs of church music and sermons on their windshield wipers. At one point, we even dropped a packet of tracts and pamphlets on lawns in the community. We were trying to let people know we were there.

And it worked. Kind of.

About a month into our community awareness campaign, I received a letter from a man who had now become aware of our church as a result of our efforts. Though I no longer have the letter, here (with some of the language removed) is essentially what he wrote

> Stop bothering me! Your people knock on my door when I'm trying to enjoy time with my family and they just want to talk about God and your Bible. After I tell them to leave, I find they've left trash about Jesus and attending your church on my doorstep. A week later, there's more trash on my lawn. When I get the mail, I find junk mail from your church. At the park last week, you left crap on my windshield.
>
> Aside from all the litter you've left lying around, the trees you've destroyed getting all this printed, and the money and time you've wasted distributing it, I feel like I'm being stalked. If this doesn't stop, I will report you and your church to the police. Leave me alone!

I remember feeling quite indignant about this letter. I thought, "If he doesn't want the stuff, why doesn't he just throw it out? Why take the time to write such a nasty letter? Does he write a letter like this to local businesses when they send him junk mail or telemarketers interrupt his dinner? I doubt it!" I took the letter to the church board and showed it to them. We all decided that one letter does not reflect the views of the entire community. We threw his letter out and continued with our campaign. We never did hear from the police.

Looking back, I think the man was right. Though it's true we were raising our "brand recognition" in the community, and our campaign did generate awareness, we got noticed for all the wrong reasons. In our attempt to reach the world, we had adopted methods of the world which contradicted the message of the gospel, and in fact, spread the wrong message about who we were and what we wanted to be. Our public awareness campaign definitely did not spread the message of the gospel.

KINGDOM MESSAGE

The message of the gospel must guide the methods that are used to spread the gospel. If we haven't got our message clear, the methods we adopt will always lead us astray. And what is the message of the gospel? It is not about politics or power. It is not about the economy or ecology. It is not about fame and glory. It is not even about how sinful the world is or how a person can get eternal life and go to heaven when they die. Though this last set of facts are truths within the gospel, they are not the main points of the gospel.

The gospel is the full-orbed message about Jesus Christ, Who He is, what He did, and how He wants us to live as a result. The gospel contains everything related to the person and work of Jesus Christ, including His birth, life, teaching, miracles, death, burial, resurrection, ascension, future return, and His ongoing life within the church as His Body.[2]

If the church is going to reveal the truth of the gospel to the world around us, we must embody the truth of the gospel in all we do and say. And since Jesus is the center of the gospel, then the message of the church must be identical to the message of Jesus. And through everything that Jesus said and did, what was the central message of Jesus? It was this: God loves the world so

[2] Jeremy Myers, "The Gospel is More than 'Faith Alone in Christ Alone'," *Journal of the Grace Evangelical Society* 20, no. 2 (Autumn 2006).

much that despite our sin, He still wants to be intimately involved in our lives. This is what Jesus announced as He walked and talked with the people of Israel. This is what He meant when He talked about the Kingdom of God. Through His life and through His actions, Jesus was telling people that God wanted to set up His rule and reign right in their midst. That God wanted to dwell with them and among them, to guide, provide, and protect them.[3]

This was the message of Jesus. It was a message of God's love and God's presence in the world.

But the method Jesus used to spread this message is revealing. Jesus is often said to be a great teacher, and He was. Teaching through sermons and lectures about the Kingdom of God, however, was secondary to the primary method Jesus used to show others that the rule and reign of God was at hand. His primary method of revealing the Kingdom was by showing through His actions what a life lived under the rule of God looked like. The primary message of Jesus was that the Kingdom of God had come, and the primary method Jesus used to spread this message was by living according to the Kingdom of God in His own life.

Let us put it another way. If someone wanted to characterize God, they could do no better than the way God described Himself to Moses: "The Lord, the Lord God, merciful and gracious, longsuffering and abounding in goodness and truth" (Exod 34:6). This is what God says about Himself. This is who God says He is.

[3] Cf. George Elton Ladd, *The Gospel of the Kingdom: Scriptural Studies in the Kingdom of God* (Grand Rapids: Eerdmans, 1959); Scot McKnight, *The King Jesus Gospel: The Original Good News Revisited* (Grand Rapids: Zondervan, 2011); N. T. Wright, *How God Became King: The Forgotten Story of the Gospels* (New York: Harper Collins, 2012).

It would follow then, that if a person is under the rule and reign of God, then their life will resemble these very same characteristics. A person who is ruled by God will be a person of mercy, grace, patience, goodness, and truth.

And how else could we describe Jesus? He was the embodiment of such traits. There is no better way of describing Him than "merciful and gracious, longsuffering and abounding in goodness and truth." That Jesus so fully fits God's self-description is not surprising, since Jesus was, in fact, God in the flesh. Theologians, with their fascination for big words, call this the "incarnation," which means "to be in the flesh." This may not be the best way of describing Jesus, since in Scripture the "flesh" if often identified with the "sinful side" of humanity, and Jesus had no sin. Nevertheless, the idea is sound: God, who is rich in mercy and love, became human in Jesus Christ. And through His life and actions, Jesus not only shows us what God is truly like, but also reveals what a true human is like. Jesus, as God in the flesh, lived according to the rule and reign of God, and gave all humanity a perfect picture of true God and true man.

Why did Jesus do this? Again, not just to give us doctrine. Nor was this a public relations campaign for God. It was not God's desire to improve His image in the world. If He had wanted to do that, He could have sent an angel, or dropped a book out of heaven onto all our lawns with the thunder booming from the clouds, saying, "Read this book!" He could have just sent miracles, and answered all our prayers. But He didn't do any of this. God wanted to show what He was like and how much He loved us, and so He came Himself. He became one of us. He took on flesh and became a man. He wanted to tangibly reveal to the world what He is like, and so He lived among us, touched our pain, healed our heartache, was present in our loneliness, and delivered us from our chains of sin and bondage.

Ultimately, of course, He died. This too, was a central part of the Kingdom message. Yet even here, we misunderstand what God was doing in Jesus. We tend to think that the death of Jesus on the cross was only to provide forgiveness as the once-for-all sacrifice for the sins of the world. That certainly is part of what Jesus accomplished on the cross, but it is by no means all that Jesus accomplished. His death on the cross is once again a way of revealing the message of the Kingdom, that the rule of God is not about power and prominence, greatness and glory, but about humility, suffering, pain, rejection, and ultimately, death. On the cross, Jesus reveals God as Someone who loves us so much, He is willing to die for us. The God revealed in Jesus is the God who suffers and dies.

Jesus came to show mankind what it looks like to live life under the rule of God. And in so doing, as the pinnacle of this expression, Jesus died. The suffering and rejection of Jesus on the cross is not a catastrophe, but a gateway to the ultimate manifestation of God and His Kingdom on earth. On the cross is where Jesus most fully reveals the nature and character of God. In Philippians 2:5-8, Paul records a Christian hymn which shows that Jesus, as a way of showing the world what it means to be God, took on humility and suffered death on the cross. It is not that Jesus died *even though* He was God, as if death on the cross went against the divine nature. No, the point of Philippians 2:5-8 is that as God, Jesus suffered and died on the cross *especially* because

He was God, because this is the way God is.[4]

The central truth of the incarnation is not that Jesus was born, but that Jesus died. As such, this truth of the incarnation should also become the central truth of the church.

INCARNATION

Just as Jesus was God in the flesh, so also the church is to be the incarnation of God. The church is commissioned to continue the incarnation in the way of Jesus, which is the way of death, the way of humility, the way of self-sacrificing service. But it seems that, like Jonah fleeing to Tarshish, we have all too often gone in exactly the opposite direction. Rather than running headlong toward humility, suffering, self-sacrifice, service, and even death, we have raced toward power, prominence, self-gratification, and self-advancement. We have adopted the methods of imperial governments, military powers, and greedy corporations. We have attempted to fight the powers of this world with their own weapons of wickedness, which they are more than willing to lend.

There are long explanations from history and psychology about why we have done this, but the real culprit is theological: we're sinners with the best of intentions. We see the influence of imperial government and the power they wield in the world, and we imagine all the good that could be done if such power could be harnessed by the church. We see the evils that military power can destroy (while ignoring all the evils it creates), and believe that similar tactics could be used to advance the cause of Christ.

[4] See Michael J. Gorman, *Cruciformity: Paul's Narrative Spirituality of the Cross* (Grand Rapids: Eerdmans, 2001).

We watch the throngs flood through the doors of amusement parks and department stores and think that if we can get such crowds to buy our wares and attend our concerts, they might be unaware when we throw the gospel into their cart as well, as if it were some blue-light special Christmas candy on December 26th.

The world notices these attempts to copy, and they are not impressed. They hear our message of incarnation, but our methods look more like a used-car salesman. Worldly methods do not help in spreading the Kingdom message. The two are incompatible, and the world sees right through it all. They hear a message of peace, love, and service, but see methods of greed, power, and glory, and understandably, they get confused. The methods and message don't mix, and the world knows it.

The church needs to be incarnational in the same way as Jesus. We need to represent God to the world, but in a way that is as close to human as possible without crossing into sin. This describes the incarnation of Jesus. He became so fully human that people had (and still have) trouble believing He was God. Similarly, the incarnational church must enter so fully into the world, and become so much like the world, that many may have trouble seeing how we are any different than the world. But that is our true secret, as it was the secret of Jesus.

ACCUSING JESUS

Certainly, we must be different than the world. Nobody argues with that. The issue is how. Once again, the example of Jesus is instructive. Though Jesus was pious, holy, and perfect, this is not what drew people to Jesus. Though Jesus was sinless, not one person in the Gospels ever comments on how holy He was. His holiness was not noticeable. To the contrary, He was often accused of drinking and eating too much, violating the Jewish Sabbath, and blaspheming God. By religious standards, Jesus was not "above reproach."

So what drew people to Jesus? It was His love and acceptance, His identification with their pain, and His willingness to go to where they were and be with them. Such things are central to the incarnation of Jesus.

With Jesus, there were no outcasts, no rejects. He never turned anybody away. He loved, accepted, and forgave everybody. He judged and condemned no one, unless it was the religious elites who had already rejected Him. With Jesus, there was no religious "insiders club." With Jesus, everybody was included. Sinners of the worst kind felt comfortable around Jesus. He even loved, accepted, and invited the religious leaders to join Him, and only had harsh things to say about them once they started trying to trap him.

Jesus became so much like the world that worldly people felt comfortable around Him while religious people did not. Worldly people invited Him to their parties while religious people accused Him of being a sinner. If this is what Jesus meant when He taught us to be in the world but not of it, we have things terribly upside down and backwards. Today, religious people are comfortable in church, while "sinners" are not.

While the church has adopted certain elements of the world to make ourselves attractive to worldly people, we did not follow the example of Jesus in becoming attractive through love, grace, forgiveness, and generosity. Instead, we mastered the worldly methods for expanding our power, multiplying our wealth, and increasing our fame. We seem to have adopted all the wrong parts.

While to be "in the world," we must become like the world, it is a fine line we must walk to keep from becoming "of the world." Like Jesus, we must adopt the things He adopted, and reject the things He rejected. Like Jesus, we must not fear the accusation of "sinner."

The secret to the ministry of Jesus is that He embraced those who would give Him a bad name, those who might mar His image in the community, and those who were cast out and rejected by all who considered themselves "godly." He recognized that the true slavery and exile was not so much to sin, but to religion which masqueraded as the way to be free from sin, but in reality just increased people's separation from God. So Jesus tore down the religious boundaries, rules, and law codes, stepped over the line of separation, and brought the love, grace, mercy, forgiveness, and freedom of God to those who were without hope in the world. Yes, He was labeled as a sinner. He was condemned, despised, and rejected. Eventually He was killed. But this also is the way of Jesus.

VISION CASTING TO DEATH

Incarnation within a dying world requires identification with the world in its pain, fear, rejection, sorrow, and ultimately, death. In this world of sin, there is no truly human existence without such things. Therefore, a desire to be incarnational requires a headlong race toward death. Yet this does not come naturally. We fight against death with all our energy. Therefore, embracing pain and death requires vision.

Many churches talk about vision casting, and this generally means envisioning how big and influential the church can be in ten or twenty years, and then deciding what steps need to be taken to get there. While it is true that "Without vision, the people perish" it is also true that the wrong vision leads people astray. The vision of most churches focuses on imagining a glorious future in which they grow and expand their ministries, programs, building size, and Sunday attendance.

Maybe the church needs a new vision—the vision of Jesus; a vision for death.

The vision of Jesus for His earthly ministry can be summarized in one word: death. From the very beginning, He set His feet on the path toward death. From very early in His ministry, Jesus began talking about His death as the reason why He came. When Satan offered Him power and the kingdoms of the world if only He would bow, Jesus refused this offer, for He knew that the path to accomplishing God's will on earth went through death. The way forward for Jesus was away from glory, away from riches, away from honor and fame.

Yet the death of Jesus was not the end of the incarnation, but the ultimate expression of it. It was in the death, the shame, the horror, and the pain of the cross where Jesus revealed a critical and crucial aspect of the character of God. Jesus revealed that God is a God who dies for the sake of others.

And so death was not the end, either of Jesus or the incarnation. It was the beginning. After three days, Jesus rose from death, and after appearing to and encouraging many of His followers, ascended into heaven and was glorified to the right hand of God the Father. This also is part of the incarnation.

The church sees the glory of the resurrected Savior, and cries out, "Yes! That is what we want! That is our vision! May the glory of God cover the earth in and through the church!" But we have forgotten that glory for Jesus only followed humiliation and death. And so it will be for the church. To go forward to glory, we must go back to death. To reach glory, we must die. Like Jesus, we must spread our arms in victorious defeat, let out a trembling sigh, and utter those words which make the devil shudder to this very day: "It is finished." Only then, once we have died, can we hope for resurrection.

Before the church can move forward, it must embrace a vision for death. So remove your life support. Turn off the iron lung. Pull the plug. Your church must die.

DESTROY THIS TEMPLE

This proposal is nothing new. It is, I believe, what Jesus Himself proposed. When He said, "Destroy this temple, and in three days I will raise it up" (John 2:19), He was not only talking about His own body (John 2:21), but also His Body, the church. When Jesus died, the temple veil was rent from top to bottom (Luke 23:45), indicating that the old system had been done away with, and the new way of life in Christ had begun, the way of worshipping the Father not in Jerusalem or Samaria, but in Spirit and in truth (John 4:20-24). The temple, with its system of priests, power, and offerings, was modeled after the political structure of palaces, kings, taxes, and tribute. Both were built upon structures where the weak and the poor served the powerful and rich. Jesus turned all this upside down, saying that "the first shall be last, and the last shall be first" (Matt 19:30, KJV).

In the hierarchical, top-down, power-first structure, Jesus championed and modeled a structure that was familiar to everybody, which was presented by God at the very beginning of time, and which is the first structure in which every person enters this world—the structure of family, of household, of kin. John Elliott, in his essay, "Temple versus Household in Luke-Acts: A Contrast in Social Institutions," writes this:

> The temple and the household constitute not simply different sites of activity but bases of different and conflicting groups of actors with differing and conflicting sets of interests and allegiances. From commencement to close of the Lukan narrative, moreover, it is the household which gradually replaces the temple as the actual sphere of God's saving presence. The temple, at first the locale of hoped for salvation and symbol of Israel's holy union with God, eventually is unmasked as the political concentration of power opposed to God's people and the truly righteous. The household, on the other hand, once the gathering place of the powerless and the marginalized, eventually emerges as the institution where God's spirit is truly active and where familial relations, shared resources, and communal values concretize the vision of salvation available to all the families of the earth.[5]

[5] Jerome H. Neyrey, ed. *The Social World of Luke-Acts: Models for Interpretation* (Peabody, MA: Hendrickson, 1991), 217. I do not quote Elliott as a defense for "house churches" nor do I believe he was trying to argue in favor of such a practice. I do not consider myself a house church proponent. I sometimes feel that "house church" is just a cheaper and smaller form of the traditional, institutional church. If you have ever attended a house church, you may have noticed that these small gatherings of believers still do most of the same things that traditional, institutional churches do, but on a lesser scale. Often, they still meet on Sunday morning for an hour or two. They still gather together in a room, sit in rows (or a semi-circle), sing songs, pray, and listen to someone teach. Then they go home until next week.

Elliott goes on to say:

> [The temple] was a system which had grown morally bankrupt. The temple, once a holy house of prayer had become a "den of thieves" (Luke 19:46). The guardians of the temple law, purity, and power had become preoccupied with status and class differentiation (Luke 11:43, 52: 15:2; 16:15; 18:11). They imposed heavy burdens (Luke 11:46), ignored the needy (Luke 10:29-37), neglected justice and the love of God (Luke 11:42), were full of extortion and wickedness (Luke 11:39), and devoured widow's houses (Luke 20:47). Jesus is credited with judging their interpretation of Torah and the cultural tradition as oppressive and self-serving (Luke 11:37-52; 16:14-15; 18:11-12; 20:9-19). Their response to criticism was violent and murderous (Luke 11:53-54; 19:47; 29:19; 21:12; 22:2, 47–23:5; Acts 3:13-15; 4:1-3, etc.). Precisely because it had failed in the *re-distribution* of not only material resources but also justice, mercy, and peace, the entire system and its chief symbol, the temple, was destined by God for destruction (Luke 11:34-35; 19:41-44; 21:5-6, 20-24).[6]

But despite this complete reversal by Jesus, despite His teachings about the death of the temple structure and system, and despite His complete rejection of the power and privilege offered to Him by the devil, the church has neglected what Jesus taught and

It is not always this way, but very frequently, there is very little real difference in the way house churches and traditional churches operate and function within the Kingdom of God. What I am proposing is the death and destruction of the whole structure. We need a fresh beginning, a new start, a way of living that looks nothing like church, but completely like Jesus. This new way is centered around families and households, but not families and households getting together to do church the same way the bigger churches do it, only smaller. We don't need that. We need something that looks more like the family of God following Jesus into the world.

[6] Ibid., 236.

modeled, has accepted the power and privilege which Jesus refused, and has almost completely reverted to the temple structure of worshipping God, a structure of expensive buildings, a powerful priestly class that speaks for God and unveils the mysteries of Scripture, a system of financial support based on tithes and offerings, and most critical of all, the wide-scale acceptance of the individualism, power, control, riches, fame, recognition, and glory which Jesus refused to accept.

So if we are really going to follow Jesus into the world, we must first follow Him into death. We must die to all the power structures and political ploys, we must cease seeking riches and fame, we must give up the goals of honor, recognition, and glory. To be the church, we must run headlong toward death and destruction.

And if that is our goal, where better to run than straight toward the gates of hell?

DISCUSSION GUIDE FOR CHAPTER 3: "THE CHURCH MUST DIE"

1. How does the world view the church? How do you think the average non-Christian would describe the average church? (If you think they view the church in mostly positive ways, you should probably go ask them.)

2. Take an honest look at your church functions and activities in the community. What sorts of things have you done which might have contributed to a negative view of your church?

3. What is God's central message to the world, and what method did Jesus use to spread this message? What is the central truth of the incarnation? How did Jesus reveal this?

4. What sort of traits should a person display who is ruled and guided by God? Do these traits match what most Christians actually reveal?

5. What drew people to Jesus? Is the church drawing people to Jesus in the same way?

6. What did Jesus believe people were truly enslaved by and how did He go about setting them free?

7. What was Jesus' vision for His ministry? Is this the same as your vision for your ministry?

8. What crucial aspect of God did Jesus reveal through His death on the cross?

Application: This chapter encourages the church to die. This suggestion was not made as a way to keep the church from being active or present in the world, but to actually encourage and *activate* our presence in the world. Future volumes of the *Close Your Church for Good* series of books will consider several practical ways that the church can die, but for now, start to creatively imagine what the church would look like without some of the tools we use to maintain our wealth, power, and control over others.

What would the church look like if it owned no buildings,

paid no clergy, and held no Sunday services? Could the church even exist without such things? What if there were no doctrinal statements, prayer meetings, and training seminars? What if we did not collect tithes and offerings and taught no membership classes?

Note that Jesus had none of these things, and so maybe, rather than helping us live and love like Jesus, such things are actually holding us back. Is this possible?

CHAPTER 4

TO HELL WITH THE CHURCH

"Some want to live within the sound of a church or chapel bell; I want to run a rescue shop within a yard of hell."
—C. T. Studd

The church should go to hell. Please do not get angry and offended at such a statement. After all, going to hell is what Jesus said we should do. If the church is going to hell, then we are headed in the right direction. To hell is where Jesus Himself went. To hell is where Jesus led His disciples. To hell is where Jesus sent the church.

In Matthew 16:18 Jesus spoke for the first time about the church He was forming. He said, "I will build my church, and the gates of hell shall not prevail against it." Far too often the church imagines that Jesus is building the church as an impenetrable fortress, with huge walls and gleaming gates, so that all the people of God can huddle together inside in safety as the forces of darkness and evil attack from outside the gates.

But that is exactly the opposite of what Jesus is saying in Matthew 16:18. He says that the gates of hell will not prevail against the church. When most Christians read this, they imagine the church as this impregnable fortress, with huge white granite walls, behind which all the people of God huddle together in safety as the forces of evil attack from outside. They think Jesus is saying that the church He is building will be a place for Christians to safely wait out the onslaught of the invading hordes of hell. They think that the church is a "safe space" to wait for the return of Jesus Christ.

But this is exactly the opposite of what Jesus says. In Matthew 16:18 Jesus says that the gates of hell will not prevail against the church. Do you see? Jesus is saying that the church He is building will go to hell, that the church will storm the gates of hell, with Jesus leading the charge. In other words, who has the gates and walls which keep out the invading army? It is not the church, but hell. And therefore, who is the invading army? It is not hell, but the church.

When you watch movies or read books about ancient warfare, do the gates of any fortress ever attack? No. Gates do not attack. Gates are built to keep invaders out. Gates are constructed to withstand the attack of an invading army outside the gates. And in Matthew 16:18, it is hell that has the gates, and these gates are under siege by the church. It is the church that has laid siege to hell. It is Satan and his minions who are huddled behind their blackened walls, hoping the gates of their dark fortress will hold.

But they will not hold. Jesus says the gates will not prevail. They will not stand. The gates of hell will fall to the invading army of the church. Just as the walls of Jericho fell before the singing and marching people of Israel, so also the gates of hell will crumble before the people of God who follow Jesus to attack the gates of hell. The "biblical story demands an offensive rather than defensive posture of the church. … An army succeeds, not through trench warfare but through movement, penetration, tactics."[1] When the church follows Jesus, Jesus will lead the church to storm the gates of hell.

So to say that the church should go to hell is not a curse upon the church; it is our marching orders. Our Leader, Jesus Christ, wants the church to follow Him to storm the gates of hell.

OUR TRUCE WITH THE DEVIL

If storming the gates of hell sounds shocking, it is because we never hear about it. The church never preaches it. Pastors ignore it. Seminaries hide it.

Why?

Because we have made a pact with the devil. As we saw in chapter 2, soon after the church laid siege to the gates of hell, Satan offered a truce, which we accepted. How did this happen?

Satan had previously made the same offer to Jesus, but He rebuffed Satan, and went on to lead the charge against the kingdom of darkness (Luke 4:1-13). After Jesus rejected the offers of Satan, Jesus announced that His mission was to find the people in chains and set them free, to seek out those who were living in darkness and bring them to light, to discover the prisons where captives were held and break their bonds, and to come to those who were broken and enslaved by the enemy and give them healing, hope, and freedom (Luke 4:18-19). Most of these people Jesus sought to rescue were held imprisoned behind the gates of hell, and so Jesus laid siege against them.

[1] Stanley Hauerwas and William H. Willimon, *Resident Aliens* (Nashville: Abingdon, 1989), 51.

However, three years into the battle, our Leader, our General, our Commander was struck down. When He died, we thought we had lost. We were disheartened. We were defeated. But three days later, our defeat turned to victory when Jesus came striding out of the gates of hell, leading many captives with Him (Eph 4:8).

Jesus gathered us together to explain what had happened and reveal the plans for the final stage in this siege. Though He had already won the war, though death and the devil had been defeated, there were still battles to be fought and captives to be freed. And though Jesus had cancelled the power of sin and escaped the clutches of hell, the gates still stood and many people were held captive behind them. So Jesus gave us His power and sent us on the mission of continuing the task He started (Matt 28:19-20; Acts 1:4-8).

For 300 years, the church continued to lay siege to the gates of hell. There were many wounded among our ranks, and numerous people fell victim to the flames and the ferocious beasts sent out to slay us. But we held strong in our resolve to continue the mission of Jesus. Jesus was with us in word, power, and deed, and though many in the church fell wounded on the field, thousands of captives were freed. The gates of hell began to crumble.

But just when the battle was almost won, tragedy struck. The worst part about it was that this tragedy was viewed by most in the church as a great victory. It happened near the beginning of the fourth century A. D. The devil came to the church, as He had come to Jesus so many years before, and congratulated us on our success. He had thought he could beat us through brute force, but we had overcome against all odds and held firm against the onslaught of his overwhelming forces. So he offered to concede to us some of what was rightfully ours. He offered to pay us tribute. He offered us power, recognition, wealth, honor, and fame.

In exchange, all we had to do was discontinue our siege against the gates of hell. We would not have to concede defeat; we could return home as victorious conquerors, complete with glory, riches, and might. We could set ourselves up as rulers of the world, calling all the nations to our beautiful and expensive centers of worship dedicated to Jesus Christ. We would have free reign to travel about and tell people about Jesus, and to preach and teach about Jesus. We could ordain our own professional priesthood, consolidate our positions of power and influence in the world, and transform the world for Jesus Christ.

All we had to do in exchange was back away from the gates of hell. Yes, there were still people trapped and enslaved behind them, but that was a small price to pay for the worldwide power and prominence that was being offered. We could do so much good with the power and money that was being offered, could we not? Though the power being offered would consume or overwhelm most other men, we believed we were wise enough to use it for good, to help the world, and to defeat the devil at his own game.[2]

So when the devil offered us his power, it did not take long for

[2] Though most do not recognize it, Frodo Baggins in The Lord of the Rings Trilogy is a beautiful picture of the church. He goes forward in weakness and smallness. Though he desires to return to the peace and tranquility of the Shire, he sets his face firmly toward the hellish fires of Mount Doom in Mordor. So also with the church. We cannot go forward in strength and power, for that is certain defeat. Nor can we sit back in the false safety of our church buildings, even when they are as beautiful as the Shire or the House of Elrond in Rivendell. We must go forward, in humility and endurance, to certain death, all for the sake of the world. This is the way of Jesus. This is the way of the church.

the church to decide. The answer was obvious. The offer was too good to pass up. We took the deal from the devil.

Almost overnight the church was transformed from a struggling band of fugitives fighting against all odds to seek and save the lost, into the richest and most powerful empire the world has ever seen. We confiscated pagan temples and converted them into centers for the worship of Jesus. We trained and hired a class of professional clergy and sent them out into the world to do the Lord's work. We passed laws and rules to support the morality taught by the church, and even made Christianity the official religion of the Empire. We set up kings and deposed them. We passed and enforced biblical laws. We controlled people's lives on earth and determined their eternal destinies as well.

As a result of all this power, Christianity entered its Golden Age. But underneath it all, behind the scenes, Satan rebuilt his walls, fortified his gates, and sent out his forces once again to enslave and capture the people of this world. The church knew this was going on, but now that they had gained power and riches, they thought that the best way to proceed was to consolidate more power and riches, until eventually the church became so rich and powerful, that nothing could stand in our way. But this pursuit has led us only further away from the gates of hell and fulfilling the mission of Jesus.

DEAL BREAKER

Where Jesus declined to meet His own needs, we have become a self-centered, needs-oriented church, asking people what they want, and then doing our best to give it to them. As we do this, more and more people come to our churches, which feeds our desire for recognition and fame—things that Jesus also rejected.

Where Jesus declined to become the ruler of the world, we have sought to gain power, dominance, riches, and control over other people and in some cases, over entire nations and countries.

For far too long we have accepted the goals and values of Satan in our attempts to establish the Kingdom of Heaven on earth. But it is not working. If we wish to rob a strongman's house, we must first tie him up. But we have entered his house and let him tie us up. By taking the power he offered, we have become his slaves.

So it is time to give it all up and return to the true mission and goal of the church. It is time to throw off our chains. It is time to rise up and fight. It is time to break the bonds that are twisted around us, pick up our holy weapons, and struggle on with the mission Jesus gave us, which we abandoned so many years ago.

It is time to break our deal with the devil, and give up our interests, glory, riches, honor, and fame, and return once again to storming the gates of hell. We must throw off everything that holds us back, and get rid of those things that so easily entangle. When we do so, it will feel like we are killing the church, but in reality, we are rising up and returning once again to the fight.

When we follow Jesus in such a way, what sort of places might we go? Where are the gates of hell and how can we storm them?

THE GOD OF DARKNESS

If we want to follow Jesus in storming the gates of hell, we must begin by looking at the world around us, and discovering the places that are filled with darkness. It is there that we will find

Jesus.

There is a picture of God in the Old Testament that sometimes troubles Christians. In various passages, God is described as being the God of darkness, or of dwelling in darkness (Ps 18:11; 97:2). Usually, we think of God as being the God of light and Satan being the prince of darkness. So how can Scripture say that our God is the God of darkness and that He dwells in darkness? Does this mean that God has an evil side? Does it mean that there is sin with God? May it never be! "God is light! In Him there is no darkness at all!" (1 John 1:5). So what does Scripture mean when it speaks of the God of darkness?

The two passages where this idea is mentioned seem to provide some clues. In Psalm 18, the Psalmist is facing death, and as he goes down into the grave, it is there, in the darkness, that He encounters God. The aspect of God that the Psalmist encounters is not the loving God of peace and love, but a God with smoke coming out of His nostrils and fire from His mouth. He sent hailstones, coals of fire, lightning, and arrows to scatter and defeat His foes. The image, it is clear, reveals our God at war. And again, where did the Psalmist encounter God in such a fashion? At the brink of death. On the edge of Sheol. At the very gates of hell. This is the same message that is taught in Psalm 97:2, the other passage which talks about God being surrounded by darkness.

The God of Darkness is a God at war. But He is not a God who battles against flesh and blood, or who wants us to seek the death of our enemies. Instead, He is a God who battles against sin, death, and evil. While the Psalmist seems to believe that his enemies are people of flesh and blood, further revelation from the New Testament reveals that our struggle is not against flesh and blood, but against principalities, powers, and rulers of the darkness of this age, and against spiritual forces of wickedness (Eph 6:12). From this we can know that when God goes to battle, it is not against humans, but against wicked spiritual forces. God battles these forces at their very doorway, at their last bastion of strength, at their last defense. God is advancing on their last stronghold at the gates of hell. If we want to see God at work in this world, one way to do this is to join Him in battle where the darkness is greatest and the evil is strongest. This is what it means to speak of our God being in darkness. He is in darkness because that is where He has gone.

The darkness does not keep God out. Where there is darkness and shadow, God is there, fighting to bring light, healing, and deliverance to those people who are there. If the church wants to join God in storming the gates of hell, in defeating the darkness, we must stop gathering in warm and comfortable rooms, with padded pews under our butts and soft music in our ears, and instead, find places in our community where we are likely to end up getting our butt kicked and leave with our ears bleeding. We must find the mean places, the dark places, the dangerous places, and take the church there. We must go to the greedy, the liars, the cheats, the thieves, and show them generosity, truth, and honesty. We must find the places that even the cops won't go, and go there with Jesus instead. Where do the most murders occur? Where do the addicts and prostitutes hang out? Let the church meet there.

HEAVEN AND HELL ON EARTH

The reason we go to the hellish places on earth is so that we can transform hell into heaven. Hell on earth can be redeemed, restored, and brought under the dominion of Jesus Christ. Just as every person who believes in Jesus for eternal life is transferred from living under the power of darkness and brought into the Kingdom of Jesus Christ (Col 1:13), so also we who have been delivered are to take the Kingdom of Heaven with us into the dark and hellish places on earth, so that those who are entrapped and enslaved can also be rescued and delivered.

We must not fall into the devilish trap of thinking that hell is only a place in the afterlife for the unredeemed. If the church is going to go to attack the gates of hell with Jesus, then this means that the gates of hell must exist here and now, on this earth, during our lives. How else could we lay siege to hell?

The truth, as indicated by Jesus Himself in Matthew 16, is that hell is here and now. Hell is a kingdom on this earth, and Jesus launched His attack on the gates of hell by inaugurating the kingdom of God on earth. We are now in the middle of a struggle between two kingdoms, and Jesus has shown us that the gates of hell will crumble and fall so that His rule and reign will cover the earth, until every knee bows and every tongue confesses that Jesus Christ is Lord (Rom 14:11; Php 2:10).

In his excellent article, "Hell is a Kingdom," Brad Jersak writes this:

> Hell is a kingdom, located wherever people are imprisoned and oppressed by the 'the powers' and death-dealers of 'this present darkness'—whether it's the military-industrial-complex, corporate or political beasts, or any personal affliction, addiction or obsession of choice. ... Jesus is not calling the death-snares of this world hades metaphorically in anticipation of the actual subterranean post-

> mortem hades. Just the opposite: the afterlife mythology of hades is a metaphor for the actual human condition 'here above.' The rhetoric or hell is less about the eschatological future and more about educating us in the 'two ways' or 'two kingdoms' competing for our allegiance here on earth.[3]

The message of the kingdom of God as taught by Jesus must be read in light of the idea that hell as a present reality. It is to the humans caught in the kingdom of hell that Jesus said, "The Kingdom of God is at hand" (Matt 4:17) This is not a promise to claim as we wait to die so we can go to heaven and spend an eternal bliss with God. This is a war cry. It is the declaration of Jesus the thief, entering into the strongman's house, to tie him up and steal his possessions. What possessions? This world and the human beings upon it (Matt 12:29).

Hell is a very real place for millions of people who live right now on earth. Children are sold into sex slavery. Women are raped. Boys are forced to march and kill as soldiers. People are infected with HIV/AIDS or other terminal diseases. Millions face the hellish existence of extreme poverty, dirty water, infection, injustice, malnutrition, abuse, neglect, and violence.

There is only one good thing about the fact that so many people live in hells like these: they can still be rescued.

So let us go! Let us stop going to church, and take the church to hell instead. Let us begin to proclaim this message: "We're going to hell! Want to come along?" or "So you want to follow Jesus? Go to hell!"

[3] Sinner Irenaeus, aka Brad Jersak, "Hell is a Kingdom: The Missing Motif Reconstructed," 6. http://www.clarion-journal.com/files/hell-is-a-kingdom-4.pdf Last Accessed June 29, 2018.

The church must find the most hellish places on planet earth, where the gates of hell are strongest, and boldly go to such places in the name of Jesus.

Who will go? Who will walk forward in the strength and light of Jesus, and batter down those blackened walls and set the captives free? This is our job, and no one else's. As we have succumbed to the lies of the devil, the church has often thought that it is our responsibility to meet the spiritual needs of people, while it is the government's job to meet the physical needs. We preach to rescue people's souls, while the government provides for their food and housing through social welfare programs.

> We preach the gospel while the government is supposed to care for the poor, the homeless, the oppressed, the disabled, or the sick …
>
> What would happen if, instead of waiting on Uncle Sam to solve social issues, the church took responsibility? What would happen if kingdom people honored Jesus' command not to own anything (Luke 14:33) and followed the kingdom principle of giving to those in need and taking in those who are without a home (Luke 6:30-31, 35-36; 10:29-37; Rom 12:13; Eph 4:28)? What would happen if wealthy suburban congregations took it upon themselves to build affordable housing for the poor? What if we actually took seriously Jesus' teaching that we are to treat everyone in need as though they were Jesus himself (Matt 25:34-46)?[4]

When Jesus taught and ministered on earth, He did not simply tell people about a sweet by-and-by, where we could go when

[4] Gregory A. Boyd, *The Myth of a Christian Nation* (Grand Rapids: Zondervan, 2005), 153-154.

we die. That is not the hope of Christianity. That is not the message of Jesus. Sure, life after death and eternal happiness with God in heaven is part of the gospel message, but it is not the only part—or even the main part.

The central message of Jesus was that in Him, heaven and earth were now being joined together. He was the nexus between God and man. In Him, heaven and earth were being rejoined and remade into one new creation of God, so that God can dwell on earth with His people, and that all might live under His rule and reign. The message and miracles of Jesus indicate that this new creation had begun. But when Jesus ascended to heaven, the Kingdom did not go with Him. It stayed behind, to be advanced by the church, the Body of Christ on earth. Jesus inaugurated the Kingdom, and He made it the task of the church to help spread the influence of the Kingdom on earth.

It is the church's task to take the Kingdom of Heaven and bear it with boldness and bravery into the meanest places on planet earth, to bring light to the darkness, healing to the sick, hope to the hopeless, and freedom to the captives. We are to spread heaven upon the earth. We must not run from sin, but run headlong towards it. This is what Jesus did. This is what the apostles did. And this is the only way to bring forgiveness, grace, and mercy to those who are in hell.

In his book, *Bringing Heaven Down to Earth,* Nathan Bierma quotes Robert McAfee Brown as saying this:

> God's message is never: Turn away from this sinful world and find me somewhere else. God's message is always: Immerse yourself in this sinful world that so desperately needs words and acts of heal-

> ing, and you will find you are not alone, for I am already there, summoning you to help me.[5]

When we go to hell to rescue and deliver those who are there, we do not go alone, for Jesus is already there, working to spread His kingdom and rescue the perishing. It is where He rescued us, and now that we have been delivered, He is calling us to return to hell with Him and rescue others.

CHURCH IS NOT SAFE

If running headlong into hell sounds dangerous, that's because it is. But Jesus never promised that following Him would be safe. Jesus never promised peace and security. Instead, He promised troubles, persecution, famine, nakedness, danger, and sword. Following Jesus to the gates of hell does not include glitz and glamour, but sweat, pain, hardship, blood, and toil.

So why does the church spend so much time, money, and energy making sure all our buildings and services are "safe"? When a church is properly following Jesus, church is anything but safe. Jesus sent the church into the middle of a warzone, right to the front lines. But when we plan a church service, we want people to enjoy their time and go home with smiles on their faces. This sounds more like a weekend holiday cruise than a desperate rescue mission. It is high time the church recognizes that we are in a battle. We are at war and the earth is our battleground. And on this field, we are not safe. War is messy, grimy, scary, and bloody.

[5] Nathan L. K. Bierma, *Bringing Heaven Down to Earth* (Phillipsburg, NJ: P&R, 2005), 89.

People get shot and wounded. Put these sorts of things on your church website for what people can expect, and then see how many people show up.

In *Attack Upon Christendom*, Søren Kierkegaard described church this way:

> We all know what it is to play warfare in mock battle, that it means to imitate everything just as it is in war. The troops are drawn up, they march into the field, seriousness is evident in every eye, but also courage and enthusiasm, the orderlies rush back and forth intrepidly, the commander's voice is heard, the signals, the battle cry, the volley of musketry, the thunder of cannon—everything exactly as in war, lacking only one thing ... the danger.
>
> So it is with playing Christianity, that is, imitating Christian preaching in such a way that everything, absolutely everything is included in as deceptive a form as possible—only one thing is lacking ... the danger.[6]

If we are going to follow Jesus, we must embrace the danger. We must run headlong into the battle where the arrows fall thickest, where the smoke blinds our eyes, and where the threat of death lies at every step. For it is here where people die every day, without light, without hope, and without love. They are trapped in a system that seeks one thing: their continued captivity and death.

> The world ... is the realm of Satan which leads it toward separation from God, and consequently toward death. That is all that it is able to do. Thus it is not for us to construct the City of God, to build

[6] Søren Kierkegaard, *Attack Upon Christendom* (Boston: Beacon, 1957), 180.

> up an "order of God" within this world, without taking any notice of its suicidal tendencies. Our concern should be to place ourselves at the very point where the suicidal desire is most active, in the actual form it adopts, and to see how God's will of preservation can act in this given situation.[7]

There are screams of people dying all around, and the church must open its eyes to the fact that nicer buildings, better sermons, longer prayer meetings, and more detailed doctrinal statements will not rescue anybody from the grip of sin and death. We must give up such things to better accomplish the mission of the church. We must die to these actions and traditions so that we might enter the hellish existence of others, thereby bringing light, life, and love into their dark world.

Great men and women of faith are formed in just such a way. Abraham was called to follow God to a foreign country, full of enemies and idol worshippers. Moses was told to return to the land which had a bounty on his head, and tell the ruler of that land to set God's people free. Joshua and Caleb saw opportunity and blessing where others saw only death and destruction. Judges like Gideon and Deborah went against all odds to deliver people from enemies and idolatry. David went out against Goliath to protect Israel from bondage and captivity. All the prophets called the people of God back to obedience, mercy, and justice despite the threats from rulers, kings, and authorities.

And just because we run headlong with Jesus into hell does not mean we will escape with our lives. We may very well die in

[7] Jacques Ellul, *The Presence of the Kingdom* (Colorado Springs: Helmers & Howard, 1989), 19.

this desperate rescue mission. But others have led the way, and we remember them as heroes of the faith.

John the Baptist was beheaded. Jesus went to the cross. Stephen was stoned to death. James the brother of Jesus was thrown off the temple tower and clubbed to death. Paul was imprisoned and beheaded. Peter was crucified upside down. Thomas was tortured, run through with spears, and then baked alive in an oven. Even today, many Christians in China, Africa, and the Middle East lose their lives as a result of following Jesus into the darkness of this world.

Following Jesus is not safe. It is full of risks, not just to our pride, power, and personal reputation, but to our very life and health. The call to follow Jesus is not a call to dignity, comfort, or respectability. It is a call to danger. True ministry does not happen when we go home with a full belly and a happy Christian tune running through our heads. True ministry happens when we feel the flames on our faces and carry the smell of smoke in our hair, when we know that every day may be our last.

In an excellent short sermon called "The Chocolate Soldier" C. T. Studd includes this little hymn, which is silently sung by many Christians of our day:

> I must be carried to the skies
> On a flowery bed of ease.
> Let others fight to win the prize,
> Or sail through bloody seas.
>
> Mark time, Christian heroes,
> Never go to war;
> Stop and mind the babies
> Playing on the floor.

> Wash and dress and feed them
> Forty times a week.
> Till they're roly-poly,
> Puddings, so to speak.
>
> Round and round the nursery
> Let us ambulate,
> Sugar and spice and all that's nice
> Must be on our slate.[8]

C. T. Studd goes on to say that we must be "Paragons of Pluck; Dare-devil Desperadoes for Jesus; Gamblers for God. Fools and Madmen" and that rather than the song above, this must be our creed:

> Learn to scorn the praise of men,
> Learn to lose with God;
> Jesus won the world through shame!
> And beckons us to His road.[9]

The idea of going into battle to "lose with God" is a shocking idea. Should not our goal be to win? No, it should not. That is what makes our battle so dangerous. We do not enter it to win, but head toward the gates of hell knowing full well that we will lose, that like Jesus, we will die.

[8] C. T. Studd, "The Chocolate Soldier." http://www.inthebeginning.com/articles/chocolate.htm. Last Accessed April 12, 2012.

[9] Ibid.

FIGHTING TO LOSE

We lose this battle because that is what Jesus did. We lose the battle because this is the only way to win.

When the church arrives at the gates of hell, we will do the same thing Jesus did in His life and ministry: We will die. We do not lay siege to the gates of hell to fight against the people we find there. We camp out at the gates of hell to love and serve the people who are trapped.

When we follow Jesus to the hellish places on earth we will die to ourselves in the process. Our dreams, our hopes, our longings, our rights, our power, our money, our prestige, our authority—all get discarded. Just as Jesus laid aside His honor and glory so that He might rescue us, He calls us to lay aside similar things so that we might rescue others.

> Though he rightfully could have demanded service and worship from all, he served the lame and the sick by healing them, the demonized by delivering them, and the outcasts by befriending them. *This* is what the kingdom of God looks like. It looks like humility. It looks like grace. It looks like service. It looks like Jesus.[10]

Loving our enemies and returning evil with good has the power to accomplish things that the weapons of war can never dream of. Someone has to stop the endless cycle of violence and hatred, and it is Jesus who showed that these things stop with Him. It is not that the downward way of Jesus into love and service "works." It usually doesn't work—at least, not as the world defines it. The reason Jesus models this way of losing rather than

[10] Boyd, *The Myth of a Christian Nation*, 35-36.

winning is because it models the way of God. God is kind to the unloving, generous to the selfish, and forgiving to the unjust. Losing our life for others "is not a stratagem for getting what we want but the only manner of life available, now that, in Jesus, we have seen what God wants."[11]

But this downward way into service and sacrifice does not lack joy, peace, and fulfillment. To the contrary, it is on the downward path, at the gates of hell, and with the redeemed people of God where the party of the Kingdom of Heaven rages most fiercely. It is here where men and angels sing and dance together to the song of the redeemed. The Warrior God swings His Sword of Truth in the rhythm of a dance that draws all people who hear it to join with Him in His creative call.

DANCES WITH WHORES

If we decide to join Jesus in storming the gates of hell, we will find something surprising when we get there. We will find a ragtag band of prostitutes, alcoholics, drug-addicts, murderers, and thieves, dancing and singing and laughing with Jesus. It is a strange sight there at the gates of hell, but it is the way of Jesus. Joy and laughter in the face of darkness and despair is one of the best ways to turn back the night and light a candle in the dark.

Jesus dances with whores, shares meals with tax-collectors, laughs at the jokes of murderers, and drinks with alcoholics.

Meanwhile, we Christians look on with disapproval. We get offended. We cross our arms and scowl at His outlandish display.

[11] Hauerwas and Willimon, *Resident Aliens*, 84.

Doesn't Jesus know what they've done? Doesn't He know He is just encouraging them? Doesn't He know how it looks to hang out with such people?

Yes, Jesus knows. He knows exactly what it looks like. It looks like the Kingdom of heaven. It looks like forgiveness. It looks like mercy. It looks like grace. Wherever Jesus goes, there is love, joy, peace, patience, kindness, goodness, faithfulness, gentleness, and self-control (cf. Gal 5:22-23). And all these things are found with Jesus as He dances with whores and killers at the gates of hell.

When we get upset at such disturbing divine behavior, we need only remind ourselves who it was that criticized Jesus for His choice of company. It was the self-righteous religious people who condemned Jesus for hanging out with tax-collectors, sinners, and prostitutes. If we feel uncomfortable hanging out with such people, might it be that we are more like Pharisees than we imagine?

> What kind of holiness does the Western Church manifest today? To answer this, we need only ask: Are the prostitutes and tax collectors of our day attracted to us or repelled by us?
>
> While there are wonderful examples of kingdom communities who attract, embrace, and transform those who are most judged and marginalized by society and religion today, on the whole today's prostitutes and tax collectors steer as far away from Christians as they did the Pharisees in the first century. Nothing could be a greater indictment of the modern Church than this.[12]

[12] Gregory A. Boyd, *The Myth of a Christian Religion* (Grand Rapids: Zondervan, 2009), 64.

CLOSING CHURCH TO BREAK HELL'S GATES

There are many in the church today who are following Jesus to hell. Shane Claiborne went to India to work with lepers, who are the rejects and outcasts of Indian society. Writing of that experience, Shane said this:

> I knew what Jesus meant when he told Peter that the 'gates of hell would not prevail' against the church, as I was finally seeing a church that was storming the gates of hell itself to save people from its horrors.[13]

Shane discovered what all great men and women of faith understand: that heaven is best found when we head toward hell, that Jesus is most active where death abounds, and that grace and mercy shine brightest in the darkness of sin. That is why he and his community, The Simple Way, sought out the worst and most crime-filled area of Philadelphia, and then moved there. In so doing, they hoped to bring redemption and transformation with them, by living in the darkness with love, mercy, and kindness.

They are not the only ones taking the church to hell. Gabe Lyons, in his book *The Next Christians*, shares the stories of numerous individuals and groups who are looking for the darkest and dirtiest places on planet earth, and then going there intentionally to share the love of Jesus with the people they find. He writes about Gary Haugen who founded the International Justice Mission to target sex trafficking. He writes about Mike Foster

[13] Shane Claiborne, *Irresistible Revolution* (Grand Rapids: Zondervan, 2006), 79.

who set up a booth at the adult entertainment expo in Las Vegas and handed out Bibles with hot pink and yellow covers with this message on the cover: "Jesus Loves Porn Stars." Gabe says that for Christians who want to bring the light of the gospel to a dark and dying world, "running away is not an option."[14]

Quite to the contrary of running away, Craig Gross argues in his book, *The Gutter*, that as followers of Jesus, the church is not supposed to simply *go to* the downtrodden and outcast, but actually *live* there. Ministering, loving, and serving those in the hellish places on earth is not a church program where we descend from our gleaming white steeples once a week or so to hand out food and pats on the back. No, as followers of Jesus, we must leave our homes of comfort and ease, and go live with those who are alone and hurting in the gutters of life. Craig writes that going to the gutter of life "isn't just a chance to take a peep around, throw out some gospel tracts, and then head home. If that's your mindset, then please don't even go at all."[15] Yes. To follow Jesus into the world means to follow Him into hell.

The church is called to go to hell. We must feel the heat of its flames, smell the smoke of its fire, see the tears of its victims, and hear their cries of pain. We must camp out at the gates of hell, and not leave until every person has been rescued. We must stay there, live there, build friendships there, and do whatever it takes to rescue people from darkness and bring them into the kingdom of God's mercy and love.

This is the radical mission of Jesus. And this is the mission of

[14] Gabe Lyons, *The Next Christians* (New York: Doubleday, 2010), 85.

[15] Craig Gross, *The Gutter: Where Life is Meant to be Lived* (Orlando: Relevant, 2005), 34.

the church. But we will find that after we have followed Jesus in this way, after we have died to ourselves and followed Jesus into hell, only then will we discover that the church has not died, but has risen to new life. Only then will light shine forth in the darkness and glory break forth like the noon-day sun. Death is not the end, but is only the beginning of the glorious new life in Jesus Christ.

So where do you see the gates of hell in the lives of your family members? Where do you see the influence and power of hell in your neighborhood? Where do you see hell in your town or city? How can you go to hell by rescuing and delivering them?

Where do you see people living in addiction, bondage, guilt, shame, and fear? Where are they abused, maligned, neglected, forgotten, overlooked, abandoned, and forsaken? Where are they sold? Where are they starving? Where are they seeking love?

Wherever you see such things, you see the gates of hell.

What is the plan of attack to charge these gates and tear them down? With Jesus at your side, these gates will not prevail against you. There are two kingdoms at war in this world, the kingdom of heaven and the kingdom of hell. Jesus is calling you to participate in one by storming the gates of the other.

Will you answer the call and go to hell with Jesus?

DISCUSSION GUIDE FOR CHAPTER 4: "TO HELL WITHI THE CHURCH"

1. What was the pact the church made with the devil?

2. What does Scripture mean when it says that God is the

God of darkness? Why is this a comforting image rather than a scary one?

3. How is hell really here on earth today? Where can hell be seen on earth today?

4. When did the Kingdom of heaven really begin? Where can it be seen on earth today?

5. How is following Jesus less like a church service and more like a war?

Application: The title of this chapter is initially shocking, but after reading the chapter, are you encouraged to take the church to the gates of hell?

It has been said that the greatest lie of Satan is that he does not exist. If this is true, the second greatest lie of Satan is that hell is only in the afterlife. This lie causes us to ignore and neglect the many billions of people who live in hell right here on earth. We walk by them every day, ignoring their cries of pain and calls for help.

And instead of follow Jesus in tearing down the gates of hell and breaking the chains of bondage, most Christians spend their time sitting in padded pews, singing feel-good songs, while sipping lattes, and having our ears tickled with a self-help sermon. But this is not where the battle rages. (Or maybe it is, but with such behavior, we're fighting on the wrong side!)

So will you listen for the trumpet call? Will you respond when the banner is raised? Will you follow Jesus to the gates of hell to help Him rescue those within?

CHAPTER 5

THE RESURRECTION OF THE CHURCH

"The way to serve Jesus, to go to meet God, has not yet been understood. People think they need to do this with churches, sermons, and worship meetings, but it is not done in this way. This way of doing things has become so rooted in us that it costs a tremendous effort to turn around and find again what will really prepare the way for the kingdom of God."
—Christoph Blumhardt

Before we can rise to new life in the future, we must die to ourselves and to our past. The church that does not die chooses instead to live in a vegetative state on artificial life support. We cling to the past, to the traditions and to the forms of church handed down to us from the eras of Constantine, the Reformation, and Industrialism. Churches that cling to these past forms are still living, but without any real life. This fight to keep from dying allows us to survive, but only as the living dead.

It is when we embrace death that we rise again to new life.

WHATEVER HAPPENED TO THE RESURRECTION?

Why don't we see resurrection today? I don't mean bodies of people actually coming forth from the grave. That is the physical resurrection which will happen when Jesus returns. We shouldn't expect to see that sort of resurrection today.

What I mean is, "Why don't we see lives of Christ-followers being radically transformed and changed into new creations?" It seems almost expected today that when a person believes in Jesus, not much will change. Oh, they might start going to church, and maybe reading their Bible and praying, and maybe if they are really zealous, they will talk about Jesus to their friends, but within a few months, old habits creep back in, old ways of living continue. Not much changes.

So whatever happened to the resurrection? Whatever happened to being raised to new life in Christ? Whatever happened to being new creations? People talk about living the "resurrected life," and sing about it, read about it, preach about it, and even pray for it, but it rarely seems to happen.

Why is this?

I believe it is because we have forgotten a vital element in the truth of the resurrection, and it is this: There can be no resurrection without death. Death always precedes resurrection. If you want to see resurrection, you must hang out with the dead. If you want to experience resurrection in your own life, you must die.

Preaching, teaching, writing, and singing about the resurrection is wonderful. It is joyful. It is happy and uplifting. But preaching, teaching, writing, and singing about death? Not so much. Yet by definition, resurrection requires death.

In fact, as you look through Scripture, you may notice that in nearly every reference to the resurrection and the new life we have in Christ, there is nearly always a reference to death as well. You cannot rise until you first have died. You must die to your old self before being raised to new life. We are buried with Christ before we are raised with Him. We must crucify the old man and the lusts of the flesh, before the new man rises from the grave.

This cycle of life is seen in the pattern of day and night, the cycle of seasons, and the following of one generation upon another. The importance of death and resurrection is the identifying characteristic of Jesus Himself, and is the central theme in all Scripture. Almost every single time God makes a promise for something great—a new son, a new nation, a new kingdom, a new restoration—the humans to whom He makes the promise try to accomplish the promise in their own strength and ability, until finally, they give up all hope and die to the promise. Only then does God step in and resurrect the shattered dream and the seemingly broken promise up out of the ashes and restore it to glorious new life. God waits until Abraham was as good as dead (Heb 11:12) before He gives Abraham a son. God sends Israel into captivity and slavery, with no hope of return and restoration, before He miraculously rescues and delivers them back to their land and rebuilds their temple (Ezra, Nehemiah).

So if we want to see the resurrection, we must die. We must die to our dreams, our ambitions, our goals, our old habits and patterns. And we must die to ourselves. Resurrection reigns only where there is death. The concept that death precedes resurrection is everywhere in Scripture, and it must be lived out through our churches as well.

So we must die. The church must not live to die, but die to live.

Many people today recognize that the church is dying, so they do everything they can to pump new life back into it. "We need nicer buildings," they say. "Better trained pastors. Exciting children's programs. Lively music. More money." But no matter what tactics are taken or which measurement we use, none of it seems to be working. Robert Farrar Capon said it best when he wrote this:

> *The church can't rise because it refuses to drop dead.* The fact that it's *dying* is of no use whatsoever: dying is simply the world's most uncomfortable way of remaining alive. If you are to be raised from the dead, the only thing that can make you a candidate is to go all the way into *death*. Death, not life, is God's recipe for fixing up the world.[1]

Many Christians, of course, look forward to dying. We love to quote Paul's words in Philippians 1:21: "For to me, to live is Christ, and to die is gain." Many Christians agree, and say they are ready to die. Death, they say, is a way to escape the toils and troubles of this world and enter into eternal peace and bliss. Dying is seen as a means to enter heaven and spend eternity with God and all their loved ones, free from pain, sin, suffering, and temptation.

When my youngest daughter was four, we were sitting at the dinner table one night when she said, "Daddy, I hope I die soon so I can go to heaven to be with Jesus." Those are shocking words to hear from a four year old, but they reflect the theology of most

[1] Robert Farrar Capon, *The Astonished Heart: Reclaiming the Good News From the Lost-and-Found of Church History* (Grand Rapids: Eerdmans, 1996), 92. Italics his.

Christians, and probably what we had inadvertently taught her ourselves. I tried to explain to her that being with Jesus is not about dying, but about living. It is not about the future by-and-by, but the present here and now. "I hope you live a very long time," I told her, "so that you can show the love of Jesus to all those around us who do not know that He loves them."

I think she understood, but it sometimes seems that few Christians understand this most basic concept about following Jesus. Jesus did not redeem and rescue us from sin and death just so that we could sit in beautiful buildings, sing beautiful songs, and listen to insightful sermons while we wait for the return of Jesus or the rapture. Church is not a pastime that helps us get through life while we wait for heaven. Church is God's plan to take the words and works of Jesus Christ to all people. Church is God's method of incarnating Jesus in every nook and cranny of this world. Jesus did not die on the cross simply so we could wait to die also. No, He died that we might live.

It is good to look forward to heaven. It is healthy to desire eternity with God. But we must do more than sing and pray while we wait for Jesus to return. While we wait, we must love and serve others, and thus bring glory to the God of the universe. As a follower of Jesus who seeks to incarnate His life among our friends and neighbors, we must not live to die, but rather die to live.

> To sit around idly waiting for Jesus to come back is neither biblical nor subversive. It's not kingdom focused and, frankly, not very compelling. The Christian life is so much more than many Christians live it. They're redeemed, so they figure they can just rest until

his return.[2]

Many of us cannot wait to die so we can be glorified; but God cannot wait for us to start living so He can be glorified. The church seems willing to die, but only to die physically so that we can "go to a better place" to be with God. This is not glorifying to God, but glorifying to death. Christoph Blumhardt said that "If all we aspire to is to get out of this world in order to be free in the next, then we pay tribute to sin and death."[3]

God wants us to die while we are living. He wants us to die to ourselves while we are alive so that before we "go to a better place" we can help this world become a better place. Jesus came to this earth not only to help bring us to heaven, but also so that He could bring heaven down to earth. The inauguration of the Kingdom of Heaven was a central theme of Jesus' life and teaching, and He wants us to continue on with the task He started, of bringing the rule and reign of God to the dark and sinful places on earth.

God put us on earth to live. It is only when we die to ourselves and die to the ways we think the world should run or the church should function, and just seek to live life with our friends and neighbors, that the Kingdom of God really begins to break forth in resurrection glory.

> In a civilization which has lost the meaning of life, the most useful thing a Christian can do is to *live*—and life, understood from the

[2] Ed Stetzer, *Subversive Kingdom: Living as Agents of Gospel Transformation* (Nashville: B&H, 2012), 88.

[3] Christoph Blumhardt, *Action in Waiting* (Farmington, PA: Plough, 1998), 192.

point of view of faith, has an extraordinary explosive force.

> ... What we need is to rediscover all that the fullness of personal life means for a man standing on his own feet in the midst of the world, who rediscovers his neighbor because he himself has been found by God.[4]

Once we have recognized the devilish influences of power, prestige, recognition, and fame, and have set our faces resolutely toward death, and have followed Jesus into hell, there is only one thing left to do: get resurrected. Of course, this is not something we can do for ourselves, but is something God does in us, which is why God wants us to die in the first place. As long as we are trying to advance the Kingdom of God through our own power and under our own resolve, we will never get anywhere. But once we die, once we recognize that there is nothing in us that can accomplish God's will on earth, we are then at the place where God can accomplish His will on earth through us.

Only once we have died and gone to the hellish places on earth can God raise us from the dead so that we can live our new life in Christ. Only once we have followed Jesus into death, giving up our dreams of grandeur and greatness, opening our hands in generosity toward others, abandoning our desire to conquer and control others, only when we have died in these ways can we begin to follow Jesus into the world, bringing light and life to others. Only once we have looked like Jesus in His death and burial can we begin to look like Jesus in His glorious resurrected life.

[4] Jacques Ellul, *The Presence of the Kingdom* (Colorado Springs: Helmers & Howard, 1989), 77-78.

LOOKING LIKE JESUS

The problem with looking like Jesus is that nobody really knows what it means. Every church in existence thinks they are representing Jesus. So while it is easy to say "The church should look like Jesus," the real questions before us are, "What does that mean? What will the church look like when it looks like Jesus? What will the church do? Where will it meet? Who will belong to it? Who, if anyone, will lead it? How will it learn? How does it serve? Whom will it serve? What will it teach?" And on and on the questions go.

The truth is that thankfully, Jesus gives great flexibility to His Body. The grace of God gives us vast freedom in our attempts to express and exhibit Christ to the world. Will this mean that sometimes a particular local church will own a building and have paid clergy who preach and perform religious rituals like baptism and the Lord's Supper? Yes, probably so.

If a particular group of believers feel that within their cultural context the best way for them to accomplish the mission of Jesus is to own buildings, hire pastors, preach sermons, and perform religious rites, then that group of believers must follow their conscience and the leading of the Holy Spirit to share the love of Jesus with others as they feel led. But at the same time, even the churches that maintain buildings and hire pastors must recognize that Jesus wants to lead the church out of the buildings and into the streets and parks of our towns to love and serve the people who are there.

If you follow Jesus in such a way, you are probably wondering what this will look like in your town or community.

The truth is that I have no idea. Nobody really knows what

church will look like ten, twenty, or a hundred years from now. Even the path to get wherever we are going is full of questions and uncertainty. In a Newsweek article about the church, Andrew Sullivan wrote this:

> I have no concrete idea how Christianity will wrestle free of its current crisis, of its distractions and temptations, and above all its enmeshment with the things of this world. But I do know it won't happen by even more furious denunciations of others, by focusing on politics rather than prayer, by concerning ourselves with the sex lives and heretical thoughts of others rather than with the constant struggle to liberate ourselves from what keeps us from God. What Jefferson saw in Jesus of Nazareth was utterly compatible with reason and with the future; what Saint Francis trusted in was the simple, terrifying love of God for Creation itself. That never ends.
>
> This Christianity comes not from the head or the gut, but from the soul. It is as meek as it is quietly liberating. It does not seize the moment; it lets it be. It doesn't seek worldly recognition, or success, and it flees from power and wealth. It is the religion of unachievement. And it is not afraid. In the anxious, crammed lives of our modern twittering souls, in the materialist obsessions we cling to for security in recession, in a world where sectarian extremism threatens to unleash mass destruction, this sheer Christianity, seeking truth without the expectation of resolution, simply living each day doing what we can to fulfill God's will, is more vital than ever. It may, in fact, be the only spiritual transformation that can in the end transcend the nagging emptiness of our late-capitalist lives, or the cult of distracting contemporaneity, or the threat of apocalyptic war where Jesus once walked. You see attempts to find this everywhere—from experimental spirituality to resurgent fundamentalism. Something inside is telling us we need radical spiritual change.
>
> But the essence of this change has been with us, and defining our

> own civilization, for two millennia. And one day soon, when politics and doctrine and pride recede, it will rise again.[5]

Andrew Sullivan says it well, but note that neither he, nor anybody else, can tell you what the church will look like in the future, or what you and your church should do specifically in your neighborhood and community.

Hopefully, each group that seeks to follow Jesus into the world will look different. One of the main problems in church history has been the desire of some churches to imitate the success of others. This has led to the rise of idol churches, where their message and methods are copied almost verbatim by others, and then reproduced and transplanted around the world, often with much less success than the original. The pastors and leaders of such copycat churches are not studying their own geographical culture, or looking at the people whom God has given them to work with, but are instead trying to emulate the culture and people of somewhere else. This shuts down the great things God is trying to do in their own unique situation.

Nevertheless, we are not left completely without guidance. Those who follow Jesus into the world will be characterized by a few universal traits due to their association with Jesus.[6]

[5] Andrew Sullivan, "Christianity in Crisis," http://www.thedailybeast.com/newsweek/2012/04/01/andrew-sullivan-christianity-in-crisis.html Last Accessed April 7, 2012.

[6] Jacques Ellul states that the church must be characterized by grace, weakness, freedom, and the Beatitudes. See Jacques Ellul, *The Subversion of Christianity* (Grand Rapids: Eerdmans, 1986), 154-173. This is challenging chapter to read, and I agree with much of what he writes.

Love

First, churches that have been raised to new life in Jesus will be known for their love. Christians should be the most loving people on earth, not just by what we say, but by what we do. People should not have to be told that Christians are loving, but should tangibly see our love in how we treat others and what we do for them daily.

One of the best ways to reveal this is not just in loving one another, but also in loving those whom others hate. In Luke 6:27-28, Jesus tells His disciples that they must be characterized by love for their enemies. They must love their enemies, bless them, and pray for them. In a world that wants the death and destruction of our enemies, those who love, bless, and serve their enemies are viewed as traitors.

In 178 A. D., a harsh critic of Christianity named Celsus said this about Christians: "What is this preference for sinners over others?" He found it incredulous that Christians seemed to prefer the sinful people in society over the upright and outstanding citizens. He found it shocking and absurd that Christians went out of their way to serve and love the rejects and outcasts in their cities. But this is the way of Jesus, is it not?

Jesus was known as the friend of tax collectors and sinners. He ate meals with them, went to parties with them, and freely forgave their sins, despite the outrage and consternation of the religious people. They thought He was betraying the righteous standards of the Law of Moses and going against all that they taught and practiced in their religion.

But Jesus behaved this way toward sinners and outcasts because this was the way God behaves towards all who are in rebellion against Him. Some of the Hebrew prophets noticed this troubling trait about God, and called Him out for it. In one place, the prophet Jeremiah tries to make sense of what He knows about God and how God seems to be blessing and loving the enemies of Israel (Jeremiah 12).

Similarly, in Job 25:3 and Psalm 145:8-9, we read that God blesses those who are His enemies and sends rain and sunshine on both the wicked and the good. In Matthew 5:45-48, Jesus says that this is what God is like and this is what He Himself is like, and so this is what those who follow Him must also be like. This is what it means to "be perfect, just as your Father in heaven is perfect." The context of this saying of Jesus indicates that perfection is primarily found in loving others—especially in love for our enemies. Love for others is a primary characteristic of the resurrected life, especially when it includes love for those the world or the church tells us to hate.

Who does this include for you? Maybe it includes homosexuals. Maybe it includes Muslim extremist terrorists. Maybe it includes members of opposing political party. Maybe it includes Republicans or Democrats. Maybe it includes Wall Street bankers or green energy activists. Maybe it is the President of the United States or illegal immigrants. Maybe it is simply your neighbor who plays his music too loud at midnight, or the coworker who keeps stealing your stapler. The point is that if we want to look like Jesus in this world, it begins with loving those we would rather hate. Loving others, especially our enemies, looks like Jesus.

Freedom

Not only will followers of Jesus be characterized by love, they will also be living examples of freedom. Jesus Christ came to this earth, not to bring us into greater bondage and enslavement, but to set us free. Many people feel that following Jesus and obeying God is too restrictive, and that God only wants to destroy our lives and give us a list of commands and instructions to follow.

Nothing could be further from the truth. It is sin that enslaves and destroys life. It is bondage to sin and addiction to things of this world that make us less than human. Jesus came to make us more human, more alive, and more free.

So when followers of Jesus go out into the world to reveal Jesus to others, they must go in a way that is compelling and beautiful. We should be the most joyful, colorful, happy, humorous, carefree, lively, and hopeful people the world has ever seen; not dour and humorless as we generally appear.

> We took a liberated community of believers living in the freedom of unqualified grace and converted it into a naval-watching institution dedicated, inevitably, to the preservation of its own structure. We created a one-eyed monster whose focus would always be on the boring rules it made for yesterday instead of on the astonishing liberty with which Christ had made it free for today. In short, we locked ourselves into the past—and then had the gall to wonder why our present always seemed so dull and our future so terrifying.[7]

Since it is for freedom that Christ has set us free, let us live fully free lives; lives free of judgment, anger, malice, despair, hate and all such things that destroy this world and destroy our lives. If we are fully committed to following Jesus, we will soon encounter His outrageous joy and be forced to decide how to handle it. If we follow Jesus into freedom and joy, our lives will become every bit as compelling and attractive to this world as Jesus was in His

[7] Capon, *The Astonished Heart*, 4.

day.

> The truth that makes us free is always ticking away like a time bomb in the basement of everybody's church. And that truth isn't a bunch of ideas. It's Jesus. Sooner or later, if we just sit still and listen, he'll blow the lid off any prison we've built.[8]

Following Jesus into freedom will look different in different situations with different people, who live in different cultures, all of whom have different gifts, desires, strengths, abilities, and who seek to love and serve different neighbors and people in different communities. But that is okay. That is the freedom we have in Jesus Christ to follow Him wherever He leads each one of us. We do not need to follow *others* in the way Jesus is leading *them*, but can rejoice in how He leads *them* while focusing our time and energy on discovering how He is leading *us*.

And it need not be anything grand. Despite our culture's propensity toward "going big" and "making a splash," most methods of advancing God's kingdom of freedom and love begin with doing whatever you can, wherever you are, using whatever you have, with the people who are around you right now. Just as the miracle of a human life begins with a single seed and a single egg, so also, the birth of the Kingdom of God in your town and your community might begin with something tiny and seemingly insignificant. In his book, *Subversive Kingdom,* Ed Stetzer provides these simple suggestions for seeing the Kingdom break into your life and neighborhood:

[8] Robert Farrar Capon, *The Mystery of Christ... & Why We Don't Get It* (Grand Rapids: Eerdmans, 1993), 140.

> Start where you are.
> Use what you have.
> Do what you can.
> And don't be afraid.[9]

Following Jesus does not require big budgets and bigger buildings. It begins with something small: An act of kindness. A word of forgiveness. A smile. A willingness to cross the street, to strike up the conversation, to ask someone how they are doing and not take "Fine" as an answer. Following Jesus means that we have the liberty and freedom to explore new ways of doing ministry with new types of people.

While the traditional ways of doing church are tried and tested, they still let a lot of people slip through the cracks. There are millions of people in our cities and towns that will never be loved or served by the traditional ways of doing church.

This is why the Kingdom of God needs people who will see the segments of our world that are getting overlooked and passed by and will step out in faith and courage to see that these other people also are shown the love of Jesus. The church needs men and women who are trying to advance the rule and reign of God in new directions to new people with new methods. Such men and women know that they have the freedom in Christ to experiment and explore. They know that while the message of the gospel does not change, the methods and means of sharing and showing this gospel must constantly change along with the culture. They know that when the methods do not change and adapt, the church becomes irrelevant, dragging the message of the

[9] Stetzer, *Subversive Kingdom*, 69.

gospel down with it.

The people who are willing to follow Jesus in new and untried ways know that the real sin is not in trying by all means necessary to save some, but in deciding that since some people do not fit into our traditional patterns they are beyond the reach of the gospel. They know that the real sin is waving the white flag at the forces of darkness who have seized control of certain segments of society and culture, and sending the secret message to Satan that as long as he leaves us alone with our comfortable pews, beautiful stained glass, and soaring steeples, we will leave him alone to do what he wants with people who are enslaved for sex, addicted to drugs, and victims of violence.

But some will not surrender to Satan. Some will not be content to sit idly by. And they will go out with love and joy, with peace and patience, with freedom and flexibility, and will storm the gates of hell to rescue those who are trapped within its dark dungeons, and bring them out to live in the light of the Kingdom of Jesus Christ. Maybe you are one of these brave ambassadors of Jesus Christ. If so, don't get shackled by the rules and traditions of a Christian religion. Instead, go forth in the freedom for which Christ has set you free.

Redemption

Once we have embraced the resurrection values of love for all people no matter what, and the freedom and flexibility to go anywhere and do anything for the sake of the gospel, the next trait of a resurrected people of God is that we will seek the redemption of all things. If the church wants to follow Jesus into the world, we must begin by looking in our town, community, and neighborhood for the places that are dark and sin-filled. Of course, this will be easy if we have followed Jesus into the hellish places on earth because they will be all around us.

But once there, we must have the courage and the faith to do what we can to help those people in those places gain freedom from their slavery to sin. They will be set free from the bondage and addiction of the kingdom of darkness and redeemed into the peace and love of the kingdom of light. When we gain the love and freedom of the resurrected life to seek the redemption of all people and all places, we soon discover that most of the "rules" of Christendom no longer apply.

For the resurrected church, there is no place off limits.

There is no place too sinful.

There is no place too corrupt.

The raging fire of the gospel of Jesus overcomes and outshines any darkness, any sin, any corruption, no matter what.

The resurrected church is not afraid of those people, places, and things that are "unclean" for we remember that He who is in us is greater than he who is in the world. We remember that as Jesus went about His ministry on earth, He went many places and did many things that would have made the typical Jewish person "unclean" by religious ritual standards, but Jesus never became defiled. Instead, He brought purity, healing, love, light, and freedom to those people and places.

Mark 5 contains a shocking series of events which clearly shows this trait of Jesus. But to understand this chapter, we must first understand the Jewish laws of purity. One of the main characteristics of the Jewish law was the constant emphasis on how to remain ritually and ceremonially clean. Almost the entire Jewish law centered around rules and regulations for maintaining a person's purity. It contains rules for where people could and could not go, what they could and could not eat, and who they could and could not touch. And if a person happened to go to one of these unclean places, eat one of these unclean foods, or touch one of these unclean people, there were elaborate and costly purification rituals that must be undertaken in order to become clean and pure again. Among these purity laws were restrictions against touching dead bodies, handling unclean animals, working with unclean Gentiles, and touching women during the times of their monthly cycle.

In Mark 5, Jesus does every single one of these things. He goes to a graveyard, which is not a place He should have been, and helps a man who lived there who was full of unclean spirits. Then Jesus sent the unclean spirits into a herd of unclean pigs that were nearby. Following this, Jesus is entreated by an unclean Gentile to come heal his daughter. On the way, Jesus is touched by a woman who has had an "issue of blood" for twelve years. This is a delicate way of saying that she had a twelve-year period, which sounds like hell on earth by any standard. After this, Jesus goes to the house of the unclean Gentile, and though his daughter has already died, Jesus touches her with His hand.

And in every single circumstance in Mark 5, it is not Jesus who gets defiled, but the person He touches who gets healed. The demon-possessed man does not defile Jesus, but Jesus heals and restores the man. The woman with the issue of blood does not defile Jesus, but is restored to full health. The deceased daughter does not defile Jesus, but is raised to new life. The point of this entire passage is that nothing of this world can taint the raging fire of redemption that burns within Jesus. When the unclean things of this world come into contact with Jesus, it is not He who gets defiled, but they which get purified and cleansed.

And the shocking truth is that the same power of redemption which coursed through Jesus also reigns in us by the power of the Holy Spirit. Let me reiterate what I said earlier: For the resurrected church, there is no place off limits. There is no place too sinful. There is no place too corrupt. The raging fire of the gospel of Jesus overcomes and outshines any darkness, any sin and any corruption, no matter what.

So we must not believe the satanic lie which says that we are safest and most secure when we remain in our holy huddle and keep at bay all who might defile our fellowship. If the Spirit of Christ is in us, then there is nothing that can defile us or make us unclean before God, for Christ has already taken upon Himself all the sin and defilement of the world and stood victorious against it. It did not defile Him, but was incinerated by the greatness and power of His purity. So we need not fear those people or places that are deemed "unclean" by others. For in Christ, we have been given permission and access to go wherever He goes, and be with whomever He desires.

Note that this redemption goes beyond just rescuing people. God's redemption through Jesus also involves all aspects of life and includes all locations of this world. Jesus not only seeks to redeem every person on earth, but also every place and event as well. Through redemption, Jesus not only transforms and rescues you and I, but also pagan holidays, wicked places, torn nations, and corrupt governments. The redemption of Jesus is all-encompassing, all-consuming, and all-inclusive.

There is no place or person on planet earth where Satan can stake his claim. There is no place where he can say, "This far and no further, for this is mine."

Through the death and resurrection of Jesus, God has once

again laid claim to every nook and cranny, every square inch, every person, every life, every event, every culture, every society, and every institution. Through Jesus, the entire world has once again come under the jurisdiction of the Kingdom of God, and the church must seek to make the Kingdom of God a reality in our lives and communities. The Kingdom will not stop advancing until every knee bows and every tongue confesses that Jesus Christ is Lord and until everything in heaven and on earth is placed under His feet.

So the church must cease allowing Satan to have his locations while we retreat into ours. We must stop the devil from taking more captives, thinking that such people and places are "beyond the hope of redemption." Rather, we must advance boldly into those places that the devil claims as his, and announce that the redemption of Jesus Christ has arrived.

When is God's power most manifested and made known? Not when we get record attendance. Not when the number of weekly Bible Studies double. Not when we construct another wing on our church building. Not when our book becomes a best seller. No, God's power is most manifested when people are set free and where this world is redeemed.

When murderers become world evangelists.

When prostitutes become role models for a Godly marriage.

When greedy businessmen become generous benefactors.

When neighborhoods filled with gang violence become loving and safe places to raise families.

When strip clubs and bars become houses of refuge and acceptance.

When war-torn nations heal and enemies come together in forgiveness.

When churches recognize that God did not save us for our own safety and comfort, but to love and serve others.

And like it or not, this sort of redemption does not primarily occur in church buildings by hearing another sermon about our freedom in Christ and singing another round of "I've Been Redeemed." No, this sort of redemption primarily occurs when the people of God go out into the sin-darkened world with the light and love of the gospel and the desire to rescue, protect, and serve the people they find. This is church. This is where Jesus leads. This is redemption.

But this is also scary. Following Jesus sometimes seems dangerous. If it doesn't, you might not be following Him.

So start slowly. Take a simple step. If you and your church have decided to take some of the suggestions in this book and are trying to decide what to do next, let me offer the same advice that is given by Robert Farrar Capon in his book, *The Astonished Heart:*

> My program would be this. Whoever was in command over the dying institution … would take the bull by the horns and kill it: close the church, dissolve the board, sequester its endowments, and sell off its property, putting the proceeds in escrow just in case the corpse ever rises and finds a use for them. Then the managers would explain to the remaining members of those churches that they were free to do anything they could think of (or nothing at all, if they so chose). A suggestion would be made, however, that they might think of holding a kind of wake on the next Sunday, perhaps in one of their homes, or in a restaurant or bowling alley that didn't open until 1:00 p.m. And if they took that suggestion …
>
> Well, they might sit and stare blankly at each other to begin with. But with any luck, some free spirit (young or old) among them

> would break the ice with the questions they had never before been able to ask—namely: "Who are we?" "Why on earth are we here?" And, most important of all, "What do we think we'd actually *like* to do?" Having no model at all to meet the upkeep on and no known shape to whip themselves into, they would for the first time be open to looking for really new answers—honest answers—that could range anywhere from "We haven't the foggiest notion, but let's get together next Sunday and see if anything's occurred to us in the meantime," to "We're here to be the church, I suppose—whatever that means," to "How about for openers we just try to stick with fellowship, breaking bread, and saying prayers?—maybe God will take care of the rest, if He wants any."[10]

This is great advice from a clergy member who has followed his own suggestions. I have tried to follow these suggestions in my own life as well, and have been led in some surprising directions. But once we have asked such questions, where do we begin to look for answers? Where do we find the guidance we need to follow Jesus into the world? How can we know where He is leading?

TRADITIONAL SOURCES OF GUIDANCE

There are numerous sources of guidance which God makes available to members of His family as they seek to spread His rule and reign on earth. The traditional forms of guidance include Scripture, prayer, the Holy Spirit, and the wise counsel of other Christians.

[10] Capon, *The Astonished Heart*, 101-102.

Scriptural Guidance

We all know we should be guided by Scripture. It is for this reason that we have Bible Studies, sermons, daily devotions, and Scripture memory. We believe that the Bible is a guide for all matters of faith and practice. Scripture as the written Word of God points us to Jesus Who *is* the living Word of God to show us how to live.

And yet even though we all agree about this, there is great disagreement on what the Bible says about what to believe and how to live. With all of the doctrinal confusion and lifestyle chaos that is in the church, some have begun to wonder whether the Bible is helpful after all. As one who has been wrestling with this issue for over a decade, I have pieced together what I believe is not so much a conclusion on the matter, but is rather a working hypothesis.

This hypothesis allows the Bible to be more authoritative and influential in our lives than ever before, while at the same time reducing the damaging, destructive, and divisive ways in which the Bible has been read, used, and taught by many Christians in many churches. This hypothesis allows the Scriptures to function as a primary guide for faith and practice, but in a way that is radically different than how the Bible is often read.

Typically, the Bible is read and taught as a sourcebook for what we should believe and how we should behave. Though no one would describe it this way, the Bible is treated as a jumbled up collection of doctrines and ethics which must be organized and categorized into neat and tidy doctrinal statements and codes of conduct. Pastors and church leaders read and study the Bible to find individual verses and passages which seem to bear significance for our lives today, and then systematize these passages into lists of what people must believe and how people must behave if they are going to belong to their church or group. In this way, the Bible is viewed as a helpful book, but only after it has been sifted, sorted, and rearranged into the kind of book which we want and which we think we need.

When read this way, the Bible functions like a doctrinal and ethical cookbook. In a cookbook, it doesn't really matter where you turn, each section is just as authoritative as any other section, and can be used to cook up recipes for others to enjoy. When the Bible is read like a cookbook, people think that all sections are equally authoritative for the life of the church, and no matter where you turn in the Bible, you can read that section of Scripture divorced from the rest of the biblical context, and cook up a nice ethical or doctrinal recipe for others to enjoy.

But what if this is not the type of book God gave us? Though many of us want this kind of book, what if the book we want is not the book God provided?

What if the Bible is *exactly* as God wanted it to be, and it does not need to be rearranged, sorted, categorized, and systematized into neat bullet points and numbered lists in order to act as a guide for following Jesus? Could it be that God knows better than we do what kind of book we need, and we have tried to change it into something more "helpful"? What if the Bible is not a cookbook, but is a story book, with a beginning, a middle, and an end, and readers which focus only on one section will miss the entire point of the narrative, as will those who mix up the beginning sections with the last sections, thinking that since they are all divinely inspired, they can go in any order we want?

A simple cursory reading of Scripture reveals what kind of book God gave us. It is clearly a story. It is a diverse story to be sure, but it is a story, with a beginning, a middle, and an end. It is a long story, a complex story, and has some odd parts such as poetry and personal letters, but these also fit in to the grand, sweeping story of Scripture. The bottom line, however, is that "The Bible is fundamentally a story of a people's journey with God."[11]

So if God gave us the kind of book He wanted, and if that book is a story, the question before us is not how we can rearrange the story and cut it up into pieces to make it more "helpful," but rather to figure out why God chose to give us such a book. Though we want a cookbook, why did God give us a story?

My working hypothesis to this question is that God knows that a story is more powerful than a list. A story has more transformative power than a doctrinal statement or an ethical code of conduct. When the Bible is taken as a story, it becomes far more powerful and effective in changing lives and transforming society than any book of doctrine or code of ethics ever could. This is true of all societies and all cultures throughout time, which makes the story of the Bible culturally relevant for all people in all places.

Once we begin to think of the Bible this way, we begin to realize that although the Bible is not the kind of book we want, it is more than sufficient for what we need. Although the Bible may be nothing more than a story, it is certainly nothing less. To try and rearrange the Bible into the type of book we want is to completely ignore and miss the universal transformative power of a well-told story. Stories can redeem, liberate, and transform people and societies better than any lists of laws or codes of ethics.

[11] Stanley Hauerwas and William H. Willimon, *Resident Aliens* (Nashville: Abingdon, 1989), 21.

And the Bible is powerful in this way because it truly is the best story ever told. If you doubt this, just start paying closer attention to nearly every movie, every novel, and every song ever written. The vast majority of them are based heavily on the themes and plotline of Scripture. The authors and writers may not have intended this, but the longings, desires, and ideas that connect with people, are the longings, desires, and ideas that are found everywhere within the story of Scripture. Yet while movies, novels, and songs often lead people astray into false directions of fulfilling their longings and desires, the story of Scripture serves as a better guide.

The story within Scripture is of mankind's quest for God, and God's quest to reveal Himself to mankind. As a story, the Bible does not tell us what to do or how to live. It tells us what people have done, how they have lived, and what the consequences were. Furthermore, the Bible shows us what people believed about God and thought God wanted from them. Ultimately, God revealed Himself to the world through the person and work of Jesus Christ.

> In Jesus we meet not a presentation of basic ideas about God, world, and humanity, but an invitation to join up, to become part of a movement, a people. By the very act of our modern theological attempts at translation, we have unconsciously distorted the gospel and transformed it into something it never claimed to be—ideas abstracted from Jesus, rather than Jesus with his people.[12]

As we read the Bible, we learn how God worked in genera-

[12] Ibid.

tions past, what sorts of endeavors the people of God embarked upon, and how these endeavors turned out. Some were successful, but others were complete failures. In this way, Scripture describes not what we must do today, but what has been done in the past as people tried to follow God in spreading His message, His rule, and His reign. We do not learn from the past what we must do today, but what they did in their time and how it turned out for them. Scripture shows us the road that was marked out for them, and how they journeyed along this road or strayed from it. Though men and women throughout history have had various ideas about who God is and what God is like, Jesus settled all the disputes and showed us who God truly is. "We are forever getting confused into thinking that scripture is mainly about what *we* are supposed to do rather than a picture of who God *is*."[13]

In his books, *The Last Word* and *Scripture and the Authority of God*, N. T. Wright uses an extremely helpful illustration for explaining how God's story functions, and where we fit into the plot.[14] He portrays history as a play with five Acts. The first four Acts of the play are (I) Creation, (II) Fall, (III) Israel, and (IV) Jesus. The book of Acts and the rest of the New Testament are the opening scenes to Act V. If I were to tweak this image a little bit, I would add Act VI from some of what we read in the book of Revelation about the New Heavens and New Earth.

Based on this, Wright argues that we are currently living in

[13] Ibid., 85.

[14] N. T. Wright, *The Last Word* (New York: HarperOne, 2006); N. T. Wright, *Scripture and the Authority of God* (New York: HarperOne, 2011). For a brief synopsis of the ideas in these books, see the paper by N. T. Wright, "How Can the Bible be Authoritative?" http://www.ntwrightpage.com/Wright_Bible_Authoritative.htm. Last Accessed May 27, 2012.

the middle of Act V, and we are actors on the stage. But there is no script, so we must improvise. However, we are not left wandering aimlessly around, blurting out whatever random line pops into our heads. No, we have Acts I-IV to guide us, and the first part of Act V to show us how the story continues, and we have Act VI to show us how the story ends. We study and learn these other Acts, not so that we can copy them scene-by-scene in Act V, but so that we can learn the plotline, the major characters, the conflict, the climax, and how the story will come to a resolution. Then, based on this information, we figure out how to get the play from the middle of Act V to the conclusion in Act VI. We might need a few cues along the way, or a few lines whispered from the wings (more on that later), but in general, if we have a good grasp of the written parts of the play that are in Scripture, it should not be too difficult to improvise our part of the story in epic fashion.

In this way, the Bible guides and informs us, not so that we mindlessly repeat what other characters in the story have said and done, but so that we allow the previous Acts in the story to inform and guide what we ourselves say and do in our part of the story. Some of the things will be similar, but most will be different, and everything will build upon what has come before to carry the plot forward toward the appropriate conclusion. Allowing the Bible to function in this way relieves the stress and burden placed on so many people to do proper "Bible study" and practice "sound hermeneutics." Certainly, these are important in their place and for certain professions, but in general, people can allow the Bible to guide them simply by reading the Bible as an ongoing story in which they have a part to play.

If it is difficult to read the Bible this way, it might be helpful to think of the Bible like a movie. When you watch a movie, whether you recognize it or not, your outlook on life is changed. Your life after you watch a movie is never the same as it was before you watched it. Sometimes the change is noticeable, and based on what you saw and heard, you resolve to live differently. Most of the time, however, the change is imperceptible, and you go on with life thinking that everything is the same. But it isn't. In ways you do not fully understand, you connect with the images on the screen, with the actions of the actors, with the plot of the story, and with the theme and ideas of the script. Consciously or subconsciously, you decide to either become more or less like some of the characters in the story, based on what they did and how the story turned out.

Like a good book or great movie, Scripture changes your life, your perspective, your imagination, and your outlook whenever you read it or think about it. The Bible does not tell us what to do; it tells us what was, what is, and what can be. When we forgive others, when we seek reconciliation and redemption, when we view others with dignity, value, and respect, when we try to incarnate God to those around us, it is not because the Bible tells us to, but because we have seen the beauty of these things in Jesus Christ, and we want others to see it too. We have beheld the glory of God in Jesus Christ, and having seen it, we desire to reflect it to others so they might see it too.

Yet there is something unique to Scripture which is unlike any movie you have ever seen or book you have ever read. By reading the Bible, God invites you *into* the ongoing story of the Bible. Though the Bible may end at Revelation 22:21, the *story* of Scripture does not end there; it carries on through each one of us in what we say and what we do. As we study Scriptural history, we learn to discern the general shape and direction that God might want to lead us in today. We learn to grasp the plot of God's story, and how we might fit into this ongoing narrative of heaven. When the Bible ends, the story does not. It invites us to carry on. It invites us to jump into the story and write our own chapter.

> Faith begins, not in discovery, but in remembrance. The story began without us, as a story of the peculiar way God is redeeming the world, a story that invites us to come forth and be saved by sharing in the work of a new people whom God has created in Israel and Jesus. Such movement saves us by (1) placing us within an adventure that is nothing less than God's purpose for the whole world, and (2) communally training us to fashion our lives in accordance with what is true rather than what is false.[15]

This is how Scripture can function for us and guide us into the way of God. As we read it, we need not look for principles, doctrines, and behaviors to copy and follow. Instead, we just read it as a story and then let the power of God's story wash over us and naturally transform and change us as only stories can. And since the Bible is God's story, concerned primarily with who God is, we will find that over time, as we read, live, and breathe in the story of Scripture, we will become ever more like God as revealed in Jesus Christ.

This is what it means to get Scriptural guidance for following Jesus into the world.

Prayerful Guidance

Aside from Scripture, prayer is another traditional form of

[15] Hauerwas and Willimon, *Resident Aliens*, 52.

guidance for Christians who seek to follow Jesus into the world. Prayer is vital and important. It is one of the primary ways we communicate with God.[16] But we must recognize that prayer is not only how God listens to us, but also how we learn to listen to our own hearts. It is through prayer that we often learn what God wants us to do, where God wants us to serve, and whom God wants us to love. We learn such things, not just so we can pray about them, but so that we can open our eyes, unfold our hands, get up off our knees, and go out and love and serve those people whom we have prayed about.

If you find yourself praying intently for your neighbor who just lost his wife, when you are done praying, go over to him with a plate of cookies and spend some time talking with him. If you find yourself praying that there would be fewer abortions in this country, when you are done praying, go get involved with a ministry which seeks to love and serve single mothers, or go volunteer at a crisis pregnancy center. If you find yourself praying for our troops overseas, when you are done praying, find out how to send them care packages. If you find yourself praying that your unsaved uncle would come to church, when you are done praying, go over to his place and start hanging out with him, spending time with him, and loving him. Rather than ask him to join you at church, you take the love of Jesus and the church to him.

This is the missing element in most Christian prayer today. We pray earnestly and fervently, knowing that Scripture tells us to pray without ceasing and that the prayer of a righteous man accomplishes much. But rarely do we follow through on our own

[16] For more on prayer, see J. D. Myers, *What is Prayer?* (Dallas, OR: Redeeming Press, 2018).

prayers, and seek to be the answer to the needs and issues we have prayed about. If you and your church are looking for ways to follow Jesus into the world, start listening to your own prayers to learn what people and needs are important to you. Then go, seeking to love and serve those people and meet those needs. In this way, our own prayers serve as a wonderful source of guidance for where God wants us to be involved in advancing His Kingdom on earth.

Holy Spirit Guidance

For many, the guidance of the Holy Spirit is a mystical and magical affair. It is believed that listening to the Spirit is only for the most spiritual of Christians, and hearing the Spirit is often accompanied by strange experiences like dreams, visions, and speaking in tongues. But such an approach to the Spirit does more damage than good. It treats the Holy Spirit as some sort of pagan deity who must rely upon ecstatic utterances and erratic behavior to get his message across to people. Many false religions depend on such things. They believe that their particular deity cannot speak to them except through such strange behavior. But our God is not like their gods.

The Spirit's voice is more like the still small voice of God which is most often mistaken for our very own thoughts. Since all who have believed in Jesus are indwelled by the Spirit of God, we must take it on faith that the Spirit Who empowered Jesus also empowers and guides us. As we go about our days, seeking to follow Jesus and love others, we must recognize that many of the thoughts that "pop into" our minds regarding the needs and concerns of others are probably not our own thoughts, but are rather due to the quiet, influencing guidance of the Holy Spirit.

Taking once again the picture of a play with five Acts, it is as if we are the actors on the stage, and the Holy Spirit is in the wings, whispering our lines to us and telling us where to go. Sometimes the whisper is so quiet it becomes difficult to hear above the applause of the crowd. Sometimes we ignore His whispers because we think we know our lines. The Holy Spirit can easily be ignored or shouted over. But with practice, the one who has attuned his heart and mind to the voice of the Spirit can hear it over any din and pick it out through all sorts of interference.

I was once with a police officer in a very crowded and noisy room. He and I were talking to each other, while at the same time his eyes kept scanning the room for any sort of problem that might arise. At one point, right in the middle of a sentence he paused, said "Excuse me," and pulled out his radio. To my surprise, rather than call for another officer on the radio, he responded to a call he had received. I had not heard a thing come over his radio. Indeed, I was having trouble hearing him even as he spoke right in front of me. But not only that, even as he was talking with the other officer, I could barely hear what the other officer was saying. My friend had the volume on his radio turned almost all the way down. It sounded like a mere whisper!

After he finished talking on the radio, I asked him how he possibly could have heard his radio with the great noise around us and with the volume turned so low. He said that years of work had trained him to tune his ears to his radio. Furthermore, he told me that while the department tries to keep radio chatter to a minimum, his brain had somehow developed the skill of tuning out all radio dialogue which had nothing to do with him or his duties. But when his name was specifically called on the radio, or the call was something that specifically concerned his responsibilities, his ears picked it up as if the voice on the radio was the only voice in the room.

I believe this is similar to learning to listen to the Spirit. There is nothing magical or mysterious about it. Hearing God is simply something that comes with time and experience. And when God speaks, a heart and mind that is in tune with the Spirit will pick up on His still, small voice, despite all the surrounding interference and distractions. Learning to listen to the guiding voice of the Spirit is essential if we are going to follow Jesus into the world with love and service toward others, and as we learn to listen, the Holy Spirit is a great source of guidance.

Guidance from Wise Christians

One final source of guidance that is traditionally accepted by Christians is the wise counsel of other Christians. When facing decisions about where to serve and how to follow Jesus, we must seek the input of others who are also following Jesus and who also seek to love and serve those whom others reject. I am not going to say much about *how* to do this since there are so many helpful books and Bible studies on the topic already.

But let me provide a warning. As we seek to gain wise counsel and guidance from other Christians, we must be on guard against copying other Christians. It sometimes seems that Christians and churches spend more time and energy following certain church leaders and churches than they do in actually following Jesus. While Jesus will lead many of us down similar roads, He will also lead different people and different churches down completely unique and diverse roads that have never before been travelled. If there is one thing that nature and history tells us, it is that God does not make clones. So we should not seek to copy the lives or ministry of anyone else.

Though scientists have just recently learned to clone sheep, the church has been doing this for a very long time. When a church or pastor becomes successful (however success is defined), we all ask how they did it. The pastor writes a book about how he grew his church from 10 to 10,000 and how you can do it too if you follow seven simple steps. Other churches try the same thing, and while some experience similar results, most fail miserably. But those who fail rarely learn that maybe God wants to do something unique and different through them. Instead, they figure they did something wrong, and when the next church-growth fad or evangelism program comes along, they once again buy the books, attend the seminars, and send people to training.

It is wise to seek the counsel and guidance of other believers, but we must never fall into the trap of believing that what God did in one church, He will also do in ours if we follow the same steps. Learning from the example of others is important, but learning from others so we can follow what they did will always hinder us from properly following Jesus.[17]

Following Jesus in this way may lead some churches and Christians in directions that look nothing like church. If so, who are we to object? There must be one focus and one focus only:

[17] Note that following Jesus is not the same thing as copying Jesus. Just as we are not to copy other churches or church leaders, so also we are not to copy Jesus. Frankly, it is *impossible* to copy Jesus, so we must not even try. Rather, just as Jesus led His disciples to do similar but different things than He had done, so also, He will lead us to do things that might be *similar* to what He did, but will have our own unique characteristics, traits, and shape. Jesus is not interested in repeating His life over and over in each believer throughout all history, but in leading us to uniquely live according to the strengths and abilities that God gave.

following Jesus in expanding the Kingdom of God in any and every direction, no matter where Jesus leads, and no matter how the mission looks. Though the following quote from Jacques Ellul is long, it is quite appropriate. Here is what he says about the formation of the church:

> [Christianity] cannot be organized. We can have neither stability, routine, collective permanence, association, nor group cohesion if we want to live by revelation, if we put [Christianity] at the center as the sole truth. It cannot be lived out socially.
>
> When we are told that the Holy Spirit constituted the church at Pentecost, we like that. But when we learn that the Holy Spirit is like the wind that blows when and where it will and we do not know where it comes from or where it is going, we do not like it. The church may say that it has the Holy Spirit, but if it does it betrays the truth and its legitimacy.
>
> When we are told that the church consists of those whom God calls, we applaud, but who are they? Who can trace the boundaries? We must say that the church has a center, Jesus Christ, but it has no circumference. We can give assurance to none and exclude none. We may believe that we have found a solution in baptism. Church members get baptized, and the baptized are the church. Well and good. But unfortunately the New Testament clearly distinguishes between the baptism of water and the baptism of the Spirit. The two do not coincide (except when the church falsely declares that they do!). We are thus back at the same difficulty.
>
> When we are told that the church has ministers, and its life is organized around them, well and good. But at once we have to remember that these ministries are a gift of the Holy Spirit and not a permanent or organized thing. This leads us to benefices with rectors

> and bishops, etc. We then fill these posts with people we think are suitable. But this is the opposite of the movement presented in the Epistles, in which the Holy Spirit gives to the church people who have the gifts of love or of the word or teaching, and the church has to find a place for them even if it had not anticipated doing so. If, after a while, the Holy Spirit does not give someone who has the spirit of prophecy but gives someone who has the gift of miracles, then the church must change its form and habits!
>
> No doubt some will reply that God is not a God of disorder, incoherence, or arbitrariness, but a God of order. Of course he is. Unfortunately the whole Old Testament shows us that God's order is not that which we conceive and desire. God's order is not organization and institution (cf. the difference between Judges and Kings). It is not the same in every time and place. It is not a matter of repetition and habit. On the contrary, it resides in the fact that it constantly posits something new, a new beginning. Our God is a God of beginnings. There is no redundancy or circularity.
>
> Thus, if His church wants to be faithful to His revelation, it will be completely mobile, fluid, renascent, bubbling, creative, inventive, adventurous, and imaginative. It will *never* be perennial, and can *never* be organized or institutionalized.[18]

Ellul is exactly right. Faithfulness to following Jesus does not result in emulation and imitation, but in vibrant creativity, graceful flexibility, joyful diversity, and visionary imagination. Yet most of our churches are not known for such things. Why not? Because although they use the traditional forms of guidance, such as Scripture, prayer, the Holy Spirit, and the wise counsel of other

[18] Ellul, *The Subversion of Christianity*, 156-157.

Christians, they have placed boundaries around the grand narrative of the Bible, have made prayer a passive monologue toward God, have tied down the Holy Spirit into a freak sideshow, and have limited the counsel of Christians to cloning the most "successful" among us. If we want to truly follow Jesus into the world, we must be willing to use these traditional sources of guidance to their fullest potential.

There is, however, one final source of guidance which is rarely recognized, and more rarely followed. The four sources of guidance looked at above are all traditional, but there is one non-traditional form of guidance that many are unaware of. This often overlooked source of guidance for following Jesus into the world is our surrounding culture.

CULTURAL GUIDANCE

Culture can also serve as a guide to help us follow Jesus. Christians often ignore culture because we think that since this world is under the control of the devil, culture also must be under his control, and therefore, just as Satan is evil, culture is evil as well. So in many cases, churches reject culture as having anything to say to us about how to follow Jesus and where He might be leading.

Theologically and practically, this is a grave mistake. The Holy Spirit is not only at work in Christians, but is also at work in the world. He is guiding history, governments, and even people who are the sworn enemies of God. By watching and observing culture and history, we can see the wind of God moving upon our times, and join with Him in His efforts. We cannot see the wind, but we can see the leaves blow and the waves form. Too often the church is busily trying to rake up leaves into nice orderly piles while the gale force winds of the Holy Spirit are intent on scatting them all over the yard. If we learn to watch where the wind blows in culture and then move with it, we will find much more success and progress in our missional endeavors.

And just like we cannot see the wind but we can see the effect of the wind, so the effects of the Spirit of God upon culture can often be viewed in the things culture produces, such as movies, music, literature, art, and politics. When gospel-related themes about justice, peace, and equality are raised in the various elements of culture, the church should suspect that these issues did not rise solely out of the hearts and minds of unregenerate people, but were created by the gentle breezes of the Spirit upon all people in our society. They often hear what the church does not.

Yet there is one thing that the culture will not include in their calls for justice, peace, and equality which only the church can provide: the centrality of Jesus and the example of the cross. The church that learns from culture will look to culture for cues, but then seek to influence and redeem culture by being something the world can never be: Jesus Christ in the world. Culture often gets condemned by Christians because although the culture raises issues of justice, peace, and equality, the motivations and end results of these goals usually result in greater injustice, war, and inequality. This happens because Christ has been left out. So the church can affirm and follow the Spirit-led stances of culture while providing for the world what it lacks: self-sacrificing love for our enemies, truth telling in all situations, honor for the weak and poor, and other Christlike characteristics which will never be practiced by culture alone.

So this is how the Holy Spirit uses culture to guide the church. The winds of the Spirit blow across the entire earth, and while the Spirit blows on the hearts and minds of Christians, the Spirit also blows on the heart and minds of others. Though discernment is required, the church can get cues as to what God is doing in the world by watching and learning from our culture. And when we see what God is doing, we can join with culture in standing against war, hunger, and other forms of inhumanity, by infusing such stands with the principles of the gospel and the example of Jesus Christ.[19]

When one studies the history of cultural evolution and the changes that have been wrought in the church, the parallels are striking. Just when the culture raises issues about slavery, so also, some voices within the church also cried out against slavery. Just when the culture starts talking about women's liberation, many voices within the church also raised their voices to the cause. Just when the culture starts asking questions about economic equality and issues of international justice for the poor, the church also started teaching and writing about similar issues.

Of course, many churches also voiced opposition to these changes in culture, but almost without fail, when the church comes down on the wrong side of such cultural issues, the voices of dissent always rise from those sorts of churches that think culture is evil and all cultural change is from the devil. This is why it is so important to watch the cultural cues. If we think that all culture is evil, we will always be on the wrong side of what the Spirit is trying to do in society and in culture.

But churches that interact with culture and recognize that God is at work in the world just as He is at work in the church,

[19] For more on this concept, see Hauerwas and Willimon, *Resident Aliens*, 46-47.

will see where the social issues of their day are rising not from the collective morality of the masses, but from the wind of the Spirit moving over the surface of the deep, seeking to bring form to the void and order to the chaos.

Some may argue, I suppose, that in these social issues, culture follows the church rather than the church following culture. Theologians and sociologists will debate who influenced whom, but I believe that trying to figure out whether the church influences culture or the culture influences the church is a bit like trying to figure out which came first: the chicken or the egg. God can use pagan kings and countries to accomplish His will, and the Spirit of God blows where He wills, so that church and culture can interact with one another to influence, challenge, and change each other for the accomplishment of the good that God intends.

We can learn much about how this works by watching the various groups in Scripture muddle their way through life while trying to serve God. When we understand the cultural and historical background to much of the development of the people of God in Scripture, here is what we see:

> They had about as much institutional structure as street theater: lots of improvisation, plenty of borrowing and stealing from whomever they bumped into, and free adaptation of other people's ideas and property for their own purposes; but precious little polity, and no property at all.[20]

Whether people realize it or not, large portions of what the Early Church said and did, came not from heavenly revelation, but from cultural emulation. They saw what was going on in the

[20] Capon, *The Astonished Heart*, 19.

culture and countries around them, and incorporated much of what they saw into their own lives and practice.

This was true of Israel as well. Much of Israel's symbols, systems, stories, rituals, routines, processes, power structures, and organizational structures were borrowed almost directly from the surrounding culture, with a few minor (but important) divinely inspired modifications.

Modern churches can do the same. We must not run from culture, but watch, observe, and learn from culture. We must believe that God is at work in culture just as He is at work in our own lives, and that the needs and issues of culture can be championed by the church.

> Christians ought to try to create a style of life which does not differentiate them from others, but yet permits them to escape from the stifling pressure of our present form of civilization.
>
> The only successful way to attack these features of our modern civilization is to give them the slip, to learn how to give them the slip, to learn how to live on the edge of this totalitarian society, not simply rejecting it, but passing it through the sieve of God's judgment.
>
> Finally, when communities with a "style of life" of this kind have been established, possibly the first signs of *a new civilization* may begin to appear.[21]

This is how the church transforms and redeems society and culture. We first learn from it and draw our cues from culture.

[21] Ellul, *The Presence of the Kingdom*, 46. Italics his.

Then we sift these cues through the guiding principles of Scripture to see what the Holy Spirit might be doing in our time and location. Finally, we live as closely as possible with the society so that we may inject it with the gospel of Jesus Christ and the overpowering influence of the Kingdom of God. When we do this, church and culture changes together, and the ways of Jesus become standard practice among all.[22]

We must remember, however, that while we can take missional cues from culture, we will not finally and completely see culture redeemed. "No, we're not going to make our world *all* better. Hate to break it to you. That's United Nations talk. That's Olympic opening ceremonies talk. That's activist groups bullhorning in the streets talk. But isn't Bible talk, nor is it reality."[23] So while we may take cues from culture and the Spirit's work within culture, we must keep our eyes on Jesus and recognize that this world will not fully and finally be redeemed until He returns to rule and reign. In the meantime, we must follow Jesus be listening to the cues He provides in Scripture, by prayer, through the Holy Spirit, from the wise counsel of other Christians, and within our surrounding culture. Doing so will give us the freedom and flexibility to follow Jesus in radical and surprising ways.

WHAT IF WE MAKE MISTAKES?

One of the biggest things holding people back from attempting

[22] Though it would take another book to show this, I believe that much of the advances in medicine, education, science, human rights, and politics are due to this infective influence of God's Kingdom in this world.

[23] Stetzer, *Subversive Kingdom*, 215.

the risky endeavor of changing the church to look more like Jesus is the fear of mistakes. We believe (wrongly) that over 2000 years, through trial and error, the church has found the best way to be the church, and it is dangerous and possibly even sinful to deviate from the tradition handed down to us.

Let us be honest. Attempting new ways of doing things *is* dangerous, and may actually lead us into mistakes, and possibly even sin. This thought of possibly leading the church into sin so terrifies some people that they attempt to change nothing, and stick instead with the tried and true methods of traditional Christianity.

The problem is that sticking with the tried and true methods of traditional Christianity may in fact be sinful as well! While it is quite possible that the tried and true methods of traditional Christianity are exactly what Jesus wanted for the church 1500 years ago, or 1000 years ago, or 500 years ago, or even 50 years ago, what Jesus wants for the church today may be *very* different. By sticking with the traditions of the past, we may be sinfully ignoring the new things that Jesus wants for today.

Similarly, though Jesus may want one local gathering of believers today to accomplish a certain task or reach a certain group of people, He may not want all believers worldwide to do those same things or reach those same people. It is a grave mistake and might very well be sinful for all Christians everywhere to copy and emulate a particularly "successful" ministry or church, even when this church comes from the traditions of the past. We are so concerned that a particular change might be sinful, we do not recognize that a *failure to change* might be the true sin.

So rather than being scared about making mistakes, we must simply own up to the fact that we are going to make them. Acknowledging this fact gives us the freedom to follow Jesus without fear. If we take a wrong path, He will bring us back. If we make a mistake, God's grace will cover that too. One thing we must not do is let the fear of sin keep us from attempting anything new or different for God as we seek to bring love, freedom, and redemption into the world. Sinning in our attempts to follow Jesus are much less grave than sinning in our attempts to play it safe. Here is what Walter Wink says about this:

> When people try to "be good Christians"—what is that but Satan's crowning victory? For "being a good Christian" is always collectively defined by some denomination or strong religious personality or creed. One does not need to "live by every word that proceeds from the mouth of God" in order to be a "good Christian"; one need only be pliant, docile, and obedient. Is it not easier to "let Jesus do it all for us," or imitate Christ, rather than embark on the risky, vulnerable, hazardous journey of seeking to find God's will in all its mundane specificity for our own lives? That harder way will certainly entail mistakes and failures, false starts, and sin masquerading as innovation.[24]

So let us follow Jesus into risky situations, for no matter what the risk, we know we will be safe, for we are following Jesus.

THE CHURCH THAT RISKS

In the Parable of the Talents, a master gives money to three of his servants and instructs them to invest the money while he is away.

[24] Walter Wink, *Unmasking the Powers: The Invisible Forces that Determine Human Existence* (Philadelphia: Fortress, 1986), 19.

We know the rest of the story. One servant turns his talent into ten, another into five, and the third plays it safe and buries his talent in the ground. When the master returns, he is pleased with the first two servants, but upset with the third. The master says that if the servant was afraid of losing the money, he should have at least put it in the bank to earn interest.

What most of us fail to remember today is that in those days, even putting money in the bank was a risky endeavor. They did not have Federal Deposit Insurance for up to $250,000. If a bank went out of business, or a shady banker ran away with the money, the depositors lost everything. So we can somewhat understand the fear of this third servant. He wanted zero risk. He feared to make any mistakes with his master's money. So he buried it.

I sometimes wish that this parable had a fourth servant, one who put the money at risk and lost it all. What would the master have said to him? Since it appears that the master operates under the principle of "Nothing ventured, nothing gained" I believe he would have been more pleased with a servant who took risks and lost everything than with the servant who took no risks at all.

But there is a reason, I believe, that this fourth servant does not appear in the parable. There is an investment secret which the master did not tell his servants, and which explains why Jesus did not include a fourth servant in His parable who risked everything and lost it all. What was this investment secret?

It was this: the master owns all the banks and businesses in town. He is the Lord of the land. The master owned a monopoly on everything. When this is the situation, there is no such thing as a failed investment. The only way the servants could have failed in their investing was if they made no investment at all—if they took no risks. That is why the master was upset with the third servant: he took no risks.

It is the same for the church. Christians today are so concerned with being the lazy third servant who buried his talent in the dirt, we use the money instead to buy a golden safe, then we tuck the remainder inside while we wait for the Master's return. We are so afraid of sinning, we take no risks. We are so afraid of failure, we make what seems to be a "safe" investment.

But in so doing, we fail to see the investment secret of the Kingdom, which is called the grace and wisdom of God. When we are trying to follow Jesus in this world, there is no such thing as a failed investment. Oh yes, it may *look* like we lose it all, but when the Master owns *everything*, it is impossible to lose *anything*. It may look like we are sinning, and indeed, maybe we do. But even there, God's grace covers our mistakes, and in His wisdom He takes our failures and turns them into His greatest success.

If your church is afraid of doing the wrong thing, or heading in a direction that may lead to sin, stop it! Frankly, if the fear of sin is holding you back, I hope you do make mistakes. Serious mistakes. I hope you take such great risks that people accuse you of sinning. For remember that religious people were always accusing Jesus of sinning. So if religious people are not accusing you of sinning, you are probably not following Jesus.

So take that risk. Step out into the void. Feel what the rush of faith does to your beating heart. Trust me: you will never be content sitting in a padded pew again.

OH CHURCH! COME FORTH!

John 11 is one of the strangest chapters in the Gospel of John. The account begins by stating that Lazarus was sick and about to die, and so his sisters, Mary and Martha, sent word to Jesus to come quickly. They thought that if Jesus came, Lazarus would not die (11:21, 32). In their urgent message to Jesus, they even reminded Him that He loved Lazarus very much (11:3).

But when Jesus receives word that Lazarus is about to die, He seems unconcerned. He basically says, "Meh ... Lazarus won't die. He'll be just fine" (11:4). This is such a strange response from Jesus that John feels he must remind the reader once again that Jesus truly did love Lazarus (11:5). John is saying, "No, really! Jesus loved Lazarus! And Mary and Martha too! I know none of you would respond this way when you hear that a loved one is about to die, but it's what Jesus said."

Yet the story gets even stranger. Immediately after reminding the reader that Jesus truly does love Lazarus, John writes that when Jesus heard that Lazarus was sick, He stayed where He was for two more days (11:6).

Wait ... *What?*

Who responds this way? If you heard that your child or spouse was about to die, wouldn't you drop everything you were doing and rush as quickly as possible to their side? Of course you would! Any human would do this. But not Jesus.

Of course, if we don't know the rest of the story, then we might think that Jesus' actions are understandable. After all, hadn't He just said that Lazarus would not die? So we are quite shocked to discover, just a few verses later, that Lazarus did in fact die. Jesus almost callously tells His disciples that they are going to go to Bethany now because Lazarus was dead (11:14). And then He says He was glad that He was not there when Lazarus died (11:15).

What kind of Savior is this? Who abandons a loved one to

death? Who makes the family of the loved one suffer alone? When He heard that His friend was sick and dying, why didn't Jesus immediately go? Even if, for some strange reason, Jesus wanted Lazarus to die, couldn't He at least have gone to the bedside of Lazarus to show His friend—along with Mary and Martha—that He cared?

After Jesus finally shows up in Bethany, Martha comes out to meet Him, but Mary stays in the house (11:20). She is not only grieving, but is probably quite hurt at the apparent indifference of Jesus. Nevertheless, when Jesus calls for Mary, she rose quickly and came to Him (11:29). How different this is than Jesus! When they called for Him, He stayed where He was for two more days, but when He calls for Mary, she quickly rises to go meet Him.

When Mary arrives, she falls at His feet and bluntly says to Jesus what we also have been feeling. She says, "Lord, if You had been here, my brother would not have died" (11:32). She is upset. She is hurt. And she is confused. So are we. What is happening here? What is going on? Why is Jesus behaving in such uncharacteristic ways?

But the odd story is not done. Only now, after Mary challenges the behavior of Jesus does Jesus begin to show some emotion. Only now, after Jesus sees Mary weeping, along with many of their Jewish friends and family, does Jesus groan in His spirit and begin to look troubled (11:33). The reader is supposed to get even more confused. We are supposed to ask, "What? *Now* He begins to show some emotion? *Now* He starts to act like He cares? Didn't He care that Lazarus was sick and dying? Didn't He know that Mary and Martha were suffering? If He really cared, He should have shown up sooner."

And then we encounter the shortest verse in the Bible. And

though many Christians see this verse as the most touching verse in Scripture, it is actually the most troubling. Jesus asks Mary and Martha to lead Him the tomb of Lazarus, and when He gets there, the text says that "Jesus wept" (11:35).

We read this and we think, "Isn't this touching? Isn't this wonderful? Look at the emotions of Jesus! He truly is human, just like us! He really loved Lazarus. He really cared for Mary and Martha." But is this really how we are supposed to read the text?

No, this is reading the text through rose-colored Christian glasses, with the added idea that "Jesus can do no wrong." Put this story in any other context with any other person, and the actions of Jesus here are quite … can I say it? … despicable. (No, I am not accusing Jesus of sin. Bear with me!)

My wife, Wendy, is actually the first one who pointed this out to me. She is one of the most insightful and honest students of Scripture I have ever known, and she has always struggled with the fact that Jesus wept in this account. As we were talking about this passage one day, she said, "Why is Jesus weeping? He knows He's going to raise Lazarus from the dead in a few minutes. Is Jesus putting on a show for the crowd?"

Have you ever wondered this? I hadn't. It didn't even occur to me. I always thought, "Well, people die when a loved one dies. This is a touching moment, because it reveals the humanity of Jesus. He wept because a loved one had died, just like we do!" Indeed, this is exactly how some in the crowd responded. When they see Jesus weeping, they say, "See how He loved him!" (11:36).

But not everyone responds this way. Some are more cynical … or confused. They say, "Yeah, well, if He had been here, He could have stopped it. What a jerk this Jesus is! If He had really loved

Lazarus, He wouldn't have waited two days before coming." In our most honest moments, we tend to agree. And then in our *really* honest moments, as seen in the question from my wife, we wonder why Jesus is weeping in the first place. "He knows He is going to raise Lazarus from the dead," we think. "So stop putting on a show as if You cared, Jesus, and just get on with it!"

Do you see? The text has been leading us to this extremely troubling aspect of the character of Jesus. Here is the question we are supposed to ask (and which *is* asked) from this text: "If Jesus cared so much, why didn't He do something in the first place … and if He *knew* He was going to raise Lazarus from the dead, then why put on a show for the crowd to make it appear that He was mourning along with them? Is God's love and concern for us just an act after all?"

I struggled with these questions for years, and then one day it hit me. The question of Mary is the same question we all have when things go wrong in life. We look at the mess our life is in, and we say, "God! Where are you? What are you doing? A little help, please! If you had stepped in here, everything would have turned out much better."

And the weeping of Jesus was not because He Himself was mourning the loss of Lazarus, or because He was putting on a show for the crowd. Jesus wept over the pain of Mary and Martha, the pain that He Himself had caused by staying away. Jesus wept because He knew that what He was doing would be misunderstood, and would cause great pain, even though the end result would bring glory to God and cause many to believe in Jesus (11:4, 15, 25-26, 40, 45).

Jesus stayed away from Lazarus so that Lazarus would die, so that God would be glorified even more through the resurrection of Lazarus, and many would be believe in Jesus, thereby joining the family of God for all eternity. But Jesus wept, because He knew that despite His good reasons, His actions had caused great pain in those who loved Him.

The exact same thing is going on with Christianity and the church. Many of us look at the state of the world, and the condition of the church, and long for the return of Jesus. We pray and call for Him to come again. But He tarries a little longer.

We cry out, "Jesus! Why aren't You coming back? Look at the mess the world is in! Look at how sick the church has become! We're dying here! Jesus! Come back! We need you now more than ever."

But He doesn't return. He stays with His friends in heaven, while we waste away here on earth.

And while He waits, I am convinced that He is weeping. Jesus weeps because He knows that His delay is causing us great pain.

We must learn from the story of Lazarus that the delay of Jesus does not mean that Jesus doesn't love us. He does. As He did with Lazarus, Jesus is delaying His return because He is waiting for us to die.

Why? Because He has better things in mind for us than what we currently experience.

Yes, His delay is painful, not only for us, but also for Him. Watching His bride suffer and die causes Him great pain because He sees how much His delay hurts us. He knows that after we die, He will raise us from the dead, and our reunion will be more glorious and happy than we can ever imagine.

Do you see what this means? It means that if we want Jesus to return, we first need to become like Lazarus, and die.

It is taught in some circles that Jesus will return once the church spreads the gospel over the face of the earth and makes the whole world "Christian." To achieve this goal, we chase after money, power, fame, glory, and influence. We think that if we can control the world, then peace will reign and Jesus will come back. What we fail to realize, and what we have learned through this book, is that all these things we chase after are only making the situation worse. The more power, fame, and control the church gains, the sicker we become.

So it is time for the church to stop sucking up the poison of power, politics, and religion. It is time for the church to stop living on life support of money, fame, glory, and influence. It's time for the church to just keel over and die.

Only then, as we lie stinking in the grave (John 11:39), will Jesus return. And the angels will say, "You know, Jesus, if you had showed up just a bit earlier, your Bride might still be alive." And Jesus will weep at the pain we went through because we did not know what was going on. But then He will lift up His eyes and pray to His Father in heaving, saying with a loud voice, "Oh Church! Come Forth!"

Then the church will rise in the power of the Spirit and the light of the Son and will go forth into this world in a way we never before imagined or thought possible. As we stand before Jesus, blinking our eyes in His glorious light, wondering what has just happened to us, He will say to those standing by, "Untie them, and let them loose into the world."

And the world will never be the same.

This is my vision for the church, as I believe it is the vision of Jesus. Jesus wants the church to die, not so that it can cease to exist, but so that it can rise again to become what He really wants and desires. Jesus wants the church as we know and practice it to drop dead so that He can call us forth to new life with Him.

So are you ready to follow Jesus into death? Don't worry; there is new life on the other side. Be willing to let the church die so that it can rise again.

DISCUSSION GUIDE FOR CHAPTER 5: "THE RESURRECTION OF THE CHURCH"

1. What always precedes resurrection? Can you get to the resurrection without going through it? So if we want the church to rise and become all that Jesus wants and desires, what must the church first do? How?

2. Too often, Christians are told that we must try to live a good life so that we can go to heaven when we die. Why is this completely opposite to what God actually wants from us?

3. What three traits will characterize the person or church that follows Jesus into the world?

4. Who is it the world is telling you to hate? Who does the church tell you to judge and reject? How can you follow Jesus in loving them?

5. Name a place, activity, or person that you think is beyond redemption. Now what is some small step you could take to shine God's light into that place, activity, or person?

6. What happens when we read the Bible like a cookbook? How else should we read it, and what will we be inspired to do when we read it this way?

7. What is the primary element that is missing in the prayer life of most Christians?

8. What is the trap we can fall into when we seek the guidance of other Christians?

9. What is the source of guidance that most Christians ignore or neglect? How do you learn about God's work in the world through this source of guidance? As you look at this source of guidance, is there anything you see God inviting you to do?

10. What is the biggest fear that holds Christians back from following God? When we understand God's love and grace for us, why is this no longer a fear?

Application: Many Christians feel like there should be "more" to their experience of church. They feel like they are missing something in their Christian life. They are right. But many of them turn to things like emotional music, miracle-working services, or special training and education to fill this spiritual void they feel. But none of these will satisfy.

The void that Christians feel comes from failing to follow Jesus into the wild and risky places of this world. As long as Christians feel that church consists of three songs and a sermon on Sunday morning, they will never step out into the world to see what God is *really* doing.

So take that risk! Embark on journey with Jesus. Boldly go where no Christian has gone before (Thank you, Star Trek!). Set out on an adventure into the great unknown. Only when you do this will you discover the Christian life you have always longed for. See how exciting life can be outside the four walls of religiosity.

AFTERWORD

I know I left you hanging at the end of the last chapter.

I'm sorry.

I called for the church to die, but I didn't really explain *how.*

After all, how can the church die so that it can rise again?

In principle, it sounds good, but how does it actually occur?

The short answer is that you look for all the ways the church seeks money, influence, power, control, fame, and glory, and then systematically strip all these elements away from the church. When you are done, the church as you know it will be dead and gone. This is the death of the church.

But from the ashes will rise the beautiful and unblemished Bride of Christ reflecting the glory of God to a watching world.

So what sorts of things need to be stripped away?

There are a myriad of possibilities, and the Holy Spirit would be happy to reveal some of them to you if you ask. But if you desire some practical examples and concrete suggestions on how "dying" might look for you and your church, you can read Volumes 2–5 in the "Close Your Church for Good" series of books.

Vol. 2: Put Service Back into the Church Service

Vol. 3: Church is More than Bodies, Bucks, & Bricks

Vol. 4: Dying to Religion and Empire
Vol. 5: Cruciform Pastoral Leadership

I look forward to joining you in one of these books, as you and I journey together by following Jesus into death, through resurrection, and ultimately into the world.

ABOUT JEREMY MYERS

Jeremy Myers is an author, blogger, podcaster, and Bible teacher. Much of his content can be found at RedeemingGod.com, where he seeks to help liberate people from the shackles of religion. He lives in Oregon with his wife and three beautiful daughters.

If you appreciated the content of this book, would you consider recommending it to your friends and leaving a review on Amazon? Thanks!

JOIN JEREMY MYERS AND LEARN MORE

Take Bible and theology courses by joining Jeremy at
RedeemingGod.com/join/

Receive updates about free books, discounted books,
and new books by joining Jeremy at
RedeemingGod.com/read-books/

SKELETON CHURCH: A BARE-BONES DEFINITION OF CHURCH (PREFACE TO THE CLOSE YOUR CHURCH FOR GOOD BOOK SERIES)

The church has a skeleton which is identical in all types of churches. Unity and peace can develop in Christianity if we recognize this skeleton as the simple, bare-bones definition of church. But when we focus on the outer trappings—the skin, hair, and eye color, the clothes, the muscle tone, and other outward appearances—division and strife form within the church.

Let us return to the skeleton church and grow in unity once again.

REVIEWS FROM AMAZON

> My church gathering is struggling to break away from traditions which keep us from following Jesus into the world. Jeremy's book lends encouragement and helpful information to groups like us. –Robert A. White

> I worried about buying another book that aimed at reducing things to a simple minimum, but the associations of the author along with the price gave me reason to hope and means to see. I really liked this book. First, because it wasn't identical to what other simple church people are saying. He adds unique elements that are worth reading. Second, the size is small enough to read, think, and pray about without getting lost. –Abel Barba

In *Skeleton Church*, Jeremy Myers makes us rethink church. For Myers, the church isn't a style of worship, a row of pews, or even a building. Instead, the church is the people of God, which provides the basic skeletal structure of the church. The muscles, parts, and flesh of the church are how we carry Jesus' mission into our own neighborhoods in our own unique ways. This eBook will make you see the church differently. –Travis Mamone

This book gets back to the basics of the New Testament church—who we are as Christians and what our perspective should be in the world we live in today. Jeremy cuts away all the institutional layers of a church and gets to the heart of our purpose as Christians in the world we live in and how to affect the people around us with God heart and view in mind. Not a physical church in mind. It was a great book and I have read it twice now. –Vaughn Bender

The Skeleton Church ... Oh. My. Word. Why aren't more people reading this!? It was well-written, explained everything beautifully, and it was one of the best explanations of how God intended for church to be. Not to mention an easy read! The author took it all apart, the church, and showed us how it should be. He made it real. If you are searching to find something or someone to show you what God intended for the church, this is the book you need to read. –Ericka

PUT SERVICE BACK INTO THE CHURCH SERVICE (VOLUME 2 IN THE CLOSE YOUR CHURCH FOR GOOD BOOK SERIES)

Churches around the world are trying to revitalize their church services. There is almost nothing they will not try. Some embark on multi-million dollar building campaigns while others sell their buildings to plant home churches. Some hire celebrity pastors to attract crowds of people, while others hire no clergy so that there can be open sharing in the service.

Yet despite everything churches have tried, few focus much time, money, or energy on the one thing that churches are supposed to be doing: loving and serving others like Jesus.

Put Service Back into the Church Service challenges readers to follow a few simple principles and put a few ideas into practice which will help churches of all types and sizes make serving others the primary emphasis of a church service.

REVIEWS FROM AMAZON

> Jeremy challenges church addicts, those addicted to an unending parade of church buildings, church services, Bible studies, church programs and more to follow Jesus into our communities, communities filled with lonely, hurting people and BE the church, loving the people in our world with the love of Jesus. Do we need another training program, another seminar, another church building, a re-

modeled church building, more staff, updated music, or does our world need us, the followers of Jesus, to BE the church in the world? The book is well-written, challenging and a book that really can make a difference not only in our churches, but also and especially in our neighborhoods and communities. –Charles Epworth

Do you ever have an unexplained frustration with your church, its service or programs? Do you ever feel like you are "spinning your wheels" when it comes to reaching others for Christ? This book helps to explain why this might be happening, and presents a convincing argument for why today's church services are mostly ineffective and inefficient. You will read concepts explained that you've not fully heard before. And you will get hints as to how it could, or should, work. –MikeM

I just finished *Put Service Back Into Church Service* by Jeremy Myers, and as with his others books I have read on the church, it was very challenging. For those who love Jesus, but are questioning the function of the traditional brick and mortar church, and their role in it, this is a must read. It may be a bit unsettling to the reader who is still entrenched in traditional "church," but it will make you think, and possibly re-evaluate your role in the church. Get this book, and all others on the church by Jeremy. –Ward Kelly

CHURCH IS MORE THAN BODIES, BUCKS, & BRICKS (VOLUME 3 IN THE CLOSE YOUR CHURCH FOR GOOD BOOK SERIES)

Many people define church as a place and time where people gather, a way for ministry money to be given and spent, and a building in which people regularly meet on Sunday mornings.

In this book, author and blogger Jeremy Myers shows that church is more than bodies, bucks, and bricks.

Church is the people of God who follow Jesus into the world, and we can be the church no matter how many people we are with, no matter the size of our church budget, and regardless of whether we have a church building or not.

By abandoning our emphasis on more people, bigger budgets, and newer buildings, we may actually liberate the church to better follow Jesus into the world.

REVIEWS FROM AMAZON

> This book does more than just identify issues that have been bothering me about church as we know it, but it goes into history and explains how we got here. In this way it is similar to Viola's *Pagan Christianity*, but I found it a much more enjoyable read. Jeremy goes into more detail on the three issues he covers as well as giving a lot of practical advice on how to remedy these situations. –Portent

This book surprised me. I have never read anything from this author previously. The chapters on the evolution of the tithe were eye openers. This is something that has bothered me for years in the ministry. It may be truth that is too expensive to believe when it comes to feeding the monster. –Karl Ingersoll

Since I returned from Africa 20 years ago I have struggled with going to church back in the States. This book helped me not feel guilty and has helped me process this struggle. It is challenging and overflows with practical suggestions. He loves the church despite its imperfections and suggests ways to break the bondage we find ourselves in. –Truealian

Jeremy Meyers always writes a challenging book ... It seems the American church (as a whole) is very comfortable with the way things are ... The challenge is to get out of the brick and mortar buildings and stagnant programs and minister to the needy in person with funds in hand to meet their needs especially to the widows and orphans as we are directed in the scriptures. –GGTexas

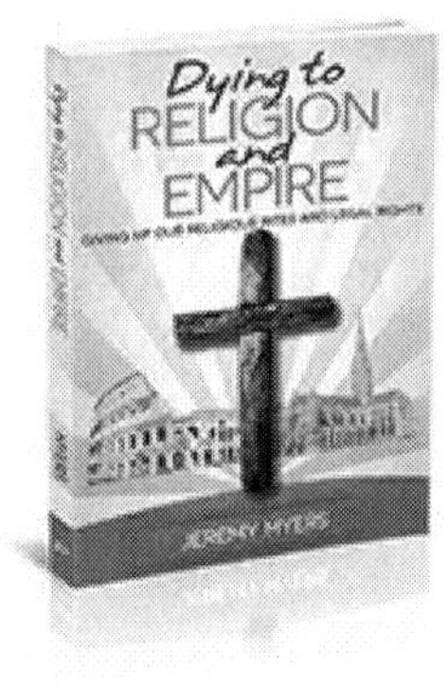

DYING TO RELIGION AND EMPIRE (VOLUME 4 IN THE CLOSE YOUR CHURCH FOR GOOD BOOK SERIES)

Could Christianity exist without religious rites or legal rights? In *Dying to Religion and Empire*, I not only answer this question with an emphatic "Yes!" but argue that if the church is going to thrive in the coming decades, we must give up our religious rites and legal rights.

Regarding religious rites, I call upon the church to abandon the quasi-magical traditions of water baptism and the Lord's Supper and transform or redeem these practices so that they reflect the symbolic meaning and intent which they had in New Testament times.

Furthermore, the church has become far too dependent upon certain legal rights for our continued existence. Ideas such as the right to life, liberty, and the pursuit of happiness are not conducive to living as the people of God who are called to follow Jesus into servanthood and death. Also, reliance upon the freedom of speech, the freedom of assembly, and other such freedoms as established by the Bill of Rights have made the church a servant of the state rather than a servant of God and the gospel. Such freedoms must be forsaken if we are going to live within the rule and reign of God on earth.

This book not only challenges religious and political liberals but conservatives as well. It is a call to leave behind the comfortable religion we know, and follow Jesus into the uncertain and wild ways of radical discipleship. To rise and live in the reality of God's Kingdom, we must first die to religion and empire.

REVIEWS FROM AMAZON

> Jeremy is one of the freshest, freest authors out there— and you need to hear what he has to say. This book is startling and new in thought and conclusion. Are the "sacraments" inviolate? Why? Do you worship at a secular altar? Conservative? Liberal? Be prepared to open your eyes. Mr. Myers will not let you keep sleeping!
>
> For all free-thinkers, for all who consider themselves "spiritual," for all who have come out or are on the way out of "Babylon," this is a new book for you! Treat yourself, buy this book and enjoy it! –Shawn P. Smith
>
> Jeremy Myers is one or the most thought provoking authors that I read, this book has really helped me to look outside the box and start thinking how can I make more sense of my relationship with Christ and how can I show others in a way that impacts them the way that Jesus' disciples impacted their world. Great book, great author. –Brett Hotchkiss

Purchase the eBook
Purchase the Paperback

CRUCIFORM PASTORAL LEADERSHIP (VOLUME 5 IN THE CLOSE YOUR CHURCH FOR GOOD BOOK SERIES)

This book is forthcoming in early 2017.

The final volume in the *Close Your Church for Good* book series look at issues related to pastoral leadership in the church. It discusses topics such as preaching and pastoral pay from the perspective of the cross.

The best way pastors can lead their church is by following Jesus to the cross!

This book will be published in early 2020.

NOTHING BUT THE BLOOD OF JESUS: HOW THE SACRIFICE OF JESUS SAVES THE WORLD FROM SIN

Do you have difficulties reconciling God's behavior in the Old Testament with that of Jesus in the New?

Do you find yourself trying to rationalize God's violent demeanor in the Bible to unbelievers or even to yourself?

Does it seem disconcerting that God tells us not to kill others but He then takes part in some of the bloodiest wars and vindictive genocides in history?

The answer to all such questions is found in Jesus on the cross. By focusing your eyes on Jesus Christ and Him crucified, you come to understand that God was never angry at human sinners, and that no blood sacrifice was ever needed to purchase God's love, forgiveness, grace, and mercy.

In *Nothing but the Blood of Jesus*, J. D. Myers shows how the death of Jesus on the cross reveals the truth about the five concepts of sin, law, sacrifice, scapegoating, and bloodshed. After carefully defining each, this book shows how these definitions provide clarity on numerous biblical texts.

REVIEWS FROM AMAZON

Building on his previous book, 'The Atonement of God', the work of René Girard and a solid grounding in the Scriptures, Jeremy Myers shares fresh and challenging insights with us about sin, law, sacrifice, scapegoating and blood. This book reveals to us how truly precious the blood of Jesus is and the way of escaping the cycle of blame, rivalry, scapegoating, sacrifice and violence that has plagued humanity since the time of Cain and Abel. 'Nothing but the Blood of Jesus' is an important and timely literary contribution to a world desperately in need of the non-violent message of Jesus. –Wesley Rostoll

So grateful to able to read such a profound insight into the Bible, and the truths it reveals, in this new book by Jeremy Myers. When reading both this book and the Atonement of God, I couldn't help but feel like the two disciples that walked with Jesus after His resurrection, scripture says that their eyes were opened…they knew Him… and they said to one another, 'Did not our heart burn within us while He talked with us on the road, and while He opened the Scriptures to us?'

My heart was so filled with joy while reading this book. Jeremy you've reminded me once more that as you walk with Jesus and spend time in His presence, He talks to you and reveals Himself through the Scriptures. –Amazon Reader

THE ATONEMENT OF GOD: BUILDING YOUR THEOLOGY ON A CRUCIVISION OF GOD

After reading this book, you will never read the Bible the same way again.

By reading this book, you will learn to see God in a whole new light. You will also learn to see yourself in a whole new light, and learn to live life in a whole new way.

The book begins with a short explanation of the various views of the atonement, including an explanation and defense of the "Non-Violent View" of the atonement. This view argues that God did not need or demand the death of Jesus in order to forgive sins. In fact, God has never been angry with us at all, but has always loved and always forgiven.

Following this explanation of the atonement, J. D. Myers takes you on a journey through 10 areas of theology which are radically changed and transformed by the Non-Violent view of the atonement. Read this book, and let your life and theology look more and more like Jesus Christ!

REVIEWS FROM AMAZON

> Outstanding book! Thank you for helping me understand "Crucivision" and the "Non-Violent Atonement." Together, they help it all make sense and fit so well into my personal thinking about God. I

am encouraged to be truly free to love and forgive, because God has always loved and forgiven without condition, because Christ exemplified this grace on the Cross, and because the Holy Spirit is in the midst of all life, continuing to show the way through people like you. –Samuel R. Mayer

If you have the same resolve as Paul, to know nothing but Jesus and Him crucified (2 Cor 2:2), then this book is for you. I read it the first time from start to finish on Father's Day ... no coincidence. This book revealed Father God's true character; not as an angry wrathful God, but as a kind loving merciful Father to us. Share in Jeremy's revelation concerning Jesus' crucifixion, and how this "vision" of the crucifixion (hence "crucivision") will make you fall in love with Jesus all over again, in a new and deeper way than you could imagine. Buy a copy for a friend—you won't want to give up your copy because you will want to read it again and again until the Holy Spirit makes Jeremy's revelation your revelation. –Amy

This book gives another view of the doctrines we have been taught all of our lives. And this actually makes more sense than what we have heard. I myself have had some of these thoughts but couldn't quite make the sense of it all by myself. J.D. Myers helped me answer some questions and settle some confusion for my doctrinal views. This is truly a refreshing read. Jesus really is the demonstration of who God is and God is much easier to understand than being so mean and vindictive in the Old Testament. The tension between the wrath of God and His justice and the love of God are eased when reading this understanding of the atonement. Read with an open mind and enjoy! –Clare Brownlee

THE RE-JUSTIFICATION OF GOD: A STUDY OF ROMANS 9:10-24

Romans 9 has been a theological battleground for centuries. Scholars from all perspectives have debated whether Paul is teaching corporate or individual election, whether or not God truly hates Esau, and how to understand the hardening of Pharaoh's heart. Both sides have accused the other of misrepresenting God.

In this book, J. D. Myers presents a mediating position. Gleaning from both Calvinistic and Arminian insights into Romans 9, J. D. Myers presents a beautiful portrait of God as described by the pen of the Apostle Paul.

Here is a way to read Romans 9 which allows God to remain sovereign and free, but also allows our theology to avoid the deterministic tendencies which have entrapped certain systems of the past.

Read this book and—maybe for the first time—learn to see God the way Paul saw Him.

REVIEWS FROM AMAZON

> Fantastic read! Jeremy Myers has a gift for seeing things from outside of the box and making it easy to understand for the rest of us. The Re -Justification of God provides a fresh and insightful look into Romans 9:10-24 by interpreting it within the context of chap-

ters 9-11 and then fitting it into the framework of Paul's entire epistle as well. Jeremy manages to provide a solid theological exegesis on a widely misunderstood portion of scripture without it sounding to academic. Most importantly, it provides us with a better view and understanding of who God is. If I had a list of ten books that I thought every Christian should read, this one would be on the list. –Wesley Rostoll

I feel the author has spiritual insight to scripture and helps to explain things. I would recommend any of his work! –Uriah Scott

I loved this book! It made me cry and fall in love with God all over again. Romans is one of my favorite books, but now my eyes have been opened to what Paul was really saying. I knew in my heart that God was the good guy, but J. D. Meyers provided the analysis to prove the text. I have been examining all the "proofs" about reformed theology because I was attracted to the message, but couldn't go all the way down the TULIP path, because it did not resonate in my heart that God who is Holy would love imperfectly. I believed Holy trumped Sovereignty, yet, I believe in the sin message, wrath of God, the Gospel and Jesus and decided that I was a "middle of the road" person caught between two big Theologies (the Big C and A). Now, I get it. I can with great confidence read the difficult chapters of Romans, and my furrowed brow is eased. Thank you, J. D. Myers. I love God, even more and am so grateful that his is so longsuffering in his perfect love! Well done. –Treinhart

ADVENTURES IN FISHING FOR MEN

Adventures in Fishing for Men is a satirical look at evangelism and church growth strategies.

Using fictional accounts from his attempts to become a world-famous fisherman, Jeremy Myers shows how many of the evangelism and church growth strategies of today do little to actually reach the world for Jesus Christ.

Adventures in Fishing for Men pokes fun at some of the popular evangelistic techniques and strategies endorsed and practiced by many Christians in today's churches. The stories in this book show in humorous detail how little we understand the culture that surrounds us or how to properly reach people with the gospel of Jesus Christ. The story also shows how much time, energy, and money goes into evangelism preparation and training with the end result being that churches rarely accomplish any actual evangelism.

REVIEWS FROM AMAZON

> I found *Adventures in Fishing For Men* quite funny! Jeremy Myers does a great job shining the light on some of the more common practices in Evangelism today. His allegory gently points to the foolishness that is found within a system that takes the preaching of the gospel and tries to reduce it to a simplified formula. A formula that takes what should be an organic, Spirit led experience and

turns it into a gospel that is nutritionally benign.

If you have ever EE'd someone you may find Myers' book offensive, but if you have come to the place where you realize that Evangelism isn't a matter of a script and checklists, then you might benefit from this light-hearted peek at Evangelism today. –Jennifer L. Davis

Adventures in Fishing for Men is good book in understanding evangelism to be more than just being a set of methods or to do list to follow. –Ashok Daniel

Purchase the eBook

CHRISTMAS REDEMPTION: WHY CHRISTIANS SHOULD CELEBRATE A PAGAN HOLIDAY

Christmas Redemption looks at some of the symbolism and traditions of Christmas, including gifts, the Christmas tree, and even Santa Claus and shows how all of these can be celebrated and enjoyed by Christians as a true and accurate reflection of the gospel.

Though Christmas used to be a pagan holiday, it has been redeemed by Jesus.

If you have been told that Christmas is a pagan holiday and is based on the Roman festival of Saturnalia, or if you have been told that putting up a Christmas tree is idolatrous, or if you have been told that Santa Claus is Satanic and teaches children to be greedy, then you must read this book! In it, you will learn that all of these Christmas traditions have been redeemed by Jesus and are good and healthy ways of celebrating the truth of the gospel and the grace of Jesus Christ.

REVIEWS FROM AMAZON

> Too many times we as Christians want to condemn nearly everything around us and in so doing become much like the Pharisees and religious leaders that Jesus encountered. I recommend this book to everyone who has concerns of how and why we celebrate Christmas. I recommend it to those who do not have any qualms in

celebrating but may not know the history of Christmas. I recommend this book to everyone, no matter who or where you are, no matter your background or beliefs, no matter whether you are young or old. –David H.

Very informative book dealing with the roots of our modern Christmas traditions. The Biblical teaching on redemption is excellent! Highly recommended. –Tamara

Finally, an educated writing about Christmas traditions. I have every book Jeremy Myers has written. His writings are fresh and truthful. –Retlaw "Steadfast"

This is a wonderful book full of hope and joy. The book explains where Christmas traditions originated and how they have been changed and been adapted over the years. The hope that the grace that is hidden in the celebrations will turn more hearts to the Lord's call is very evident. Jeremy Myers has given us a lovely gift this Christmas. His insights will lift our hearts and remain with us a long time. –Janet Cardoza

I love how the author uses multiple sources to back up his opinions. He doesn't just use bible verses, he goes back into the history of the topics (pagan rituals, Santa, etc.) as well. Great book! –Jenna G.

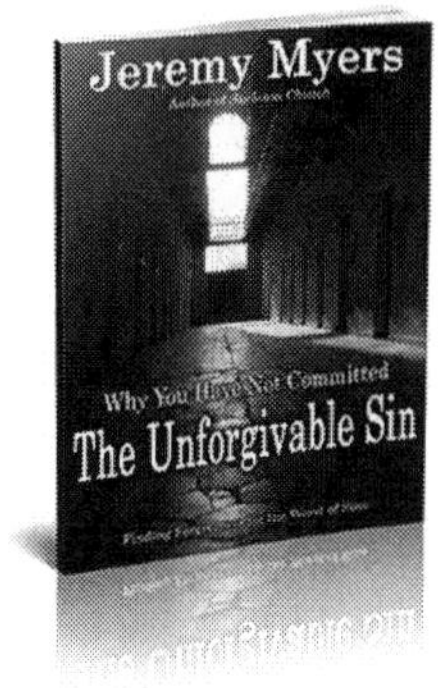

WHY YOU HAVE NOT COMMITTED THE UNFORGIVABLE SIN: FINDING FORGIVENESS FOR THE WORST OF SINS

Are you afraid that you have committed the unforgivable sin?

In this book, you will learn what this sin is and why you have not committed it. After surveying the various views about blasphemy against the Holy Spirit and examining Matthew 12:31-32, you will learn what the sin is and how it is committed.

As a result of reading this book, you will gain freedom from the fear of committing the worst of all sins, and learn how much God loves you!

REVIEWS FROM AMAZON

> This book addressed things I have struggled and felt pandered to for years, and helped to bring wholeness to my heart again. –Natalie Fleming

> A great read, on a controversial subject; biblical, historical and contextually treated to give the greatest understanding. May be the best on this subject (and there is very few) ever written. – Tony Vance

> You must read this book. Forgiveness is necessary to see your blessings. So if you purchase this book, [you will have] no regrets. –Virtuous Woman

> Jeremy Myers covers this most difficult topic thoroughly and with

great compassion. –J. Holland

Good study. Very helpful. A must read. I like this study because it was an in depth study of the scripture. –Rose Knowles

Excellent read and helpful the reader offers hope for all who may be effected by this subject. He includes e-mails from people, [and] is very thorough. –Richie

Wonderful explication of the unpardonable sin. God loves you more than you know. May Jesus Christ be with you always. –Robert M Sawin III

Excellent book! Highly recommend for anyone who has anxiety and fear about having committed the unforgivable sin. –William Tom

As someone who is constantly worried that they have disappointed or offended God, this book was, quite literally, a "Godsend." I thought I had committed this sin as I swore against the Holy Spirit in my mind. It only started after reading the verse about it in the Bible. The swear words against Him came into my mind over and over and I couldn't seem to stop no matter how much I prayed. I was convinced I was going to hell and cried constantly. I was extremely worried and depressed. This book has allowed me to breathe again, to have hope again. Thank you, Jeremy. I will read and re-read. I believe this book was definitely God inspired. I only wish I had found it sooner. –Sue

BOOK PUBLISHING INSTRUCTIONS: A STEP-BY-STEP GUIDE TO PUBLISHING YOUR BOOK AS A PAPERBACK AND EBOOK

The dirty little secret of the publishing industry is that authors don't really need publishing companies any longer. If you want to get published, you can!

This book gives you everything you need to take your unfinished manuscript and get it into print and into the hands of readers. It shows you how to format your manuscript for printing as a paperback and preparing the files for digital eReaders like the Kindle, iPad, and Nook.

This book provides tips and suggestions for editing and typesetting your book, inserting interior images, designing a book cover, and even marketing your book so that people will buy it and read it. Detailed descriptions of what to do are accompanied by screenshots for each step. Additional tools, tips, and websites are also provided which will help get your book published.

If you have a book idea, you need to read this book.

REVIEWS FROM AMAZON

> I self-published my first book with the "assistance" of a publishing company. In the end I was extremely unhappy for various reasons

… Jeremy Myers' book … does not try to impress with all kinds of "learned quotations" but gets right to the thrust of things, plain and simple. For me this book will be a constant companion as I work on a considerable list of books on Christian doctrines. Whether you are a new aspiring author or one with a book or so behind you, save yourself much effort and frustration by investing in this book.
–Gerrie Malan

This book was incredibly helpful. I am in the process of writing my first book and the info in here has really helped me go into this process with a plan. I now realize how incredibly naive I was about what goes into publishing a book, yet instead of feeling overwhelmed, I now feel prepared for the task. Jeremy has laid out the steps to every aspect of publishing step by step as though they were recipes in a cook book. From writing with Styles and using the Style guide to incorporating images and page layouts, it is all there and will end up saving you hours of time in the editing phase.
–W. Rostoll

THE LIE – A SHORT STORY

When one billion people disappear from earth, what explanation does the president provide? Is he telling the truth, or exposing an age-old lie?

This fictional short story contains his televised speech.

Have you ever wondered what the antichrist will say when a billion people disappear from planet earth at the rapture? Here is a fictional account of what he might say.

Purchase the eBook for $0.99

JOIN JEREMY MYERS AND LEARN MORE

Take Bible and theology courses by joining Jeremy at RedeemingGod.com/join/

Receive updates about free books, discounted books, and new books by joining Jeremy at RedeemingGod.com/read-books/

Printed in Great Britain
by Amazon

42553456R00108